The Next of Kin: Those who Wait and Wonder

by Nellie L. McClung

FOREWORD

It was a bleak day in November, with a thick, gray sky, and a great, noisy, blustering wind that had a knack of facing you, no matter which way you were going; a wind that would be in ill-favor anywhere, but in northern Alberta, where the wind is not due to blow at all, it was what the really polite people call "impossible." Those who were not so polite called it something quite different, but the meaning is the same.

There are districts, not so very far from us, where the wind blows so constantly that the people grow accustomed to it; they depend on it; some say they like it; and when by a rare chance it goes down for a few hours, they become nervous, panicky, and apprehensive, always listening, expecting something to happen. But we of the windless North, with our sunlit spaces, our quiet days and nights, grow peevish, petulant, and full of grouch when the wind blows. We will stand anything but that. We resent wind; it is not in the bond; we will have none of it!

"You won't have many at the meeting to-day," said the station agent cheerfully, when I went into the small waiting-room to wait for the President of the Red Cross Society, who wanted to see me before the meeting. "No, you won't have many a day like this, although there are some who will come out, wind or no wind, to hear a woman speak—it's just idle curiosity, that's all it is."

"Oh, come," I said, "be generous; maybe they really think that she may have something to say!"

"Well, you see," said this amateur philosopher, as he dusted the gray-painted sill of the wicket with a large red-and-white handkerchief, "it *is* great to hear a woman speak in public, anyway, even if she does not do it very well. It's sorto' like seeing a pony walking on its hind legs; it's clever even if it's not natural. You will have some all right—I'm going over myself. There would have been a big crowd in if it hadn't been for the wind. You see, you've never been here before and that all helps."

Then the President of the Red Cross Society came and conducted me to the house quite near the station where I was to be entertained. My hostess, who came to the door herself in answer to our ring, was a sweet-faced, little Southern woman transplanted here in northern Canada, who with true Southern hospitality and thoughtfulness asked me if I would not like to step right upstairs and "handsome up a bit" before I went to the meeting,—"not but what you're looking right peart," she added quickly.

3

When I was shown upstairs to the spare room and was well into the business of "handsoming up," I heard a small voice at the door speaking my name. I opened the door and found there a small girl of about seven years of age, who timidly asked if she might come in. I told her that I was just dressing and would be glad to have her at some other time. But she quickly assured me that it was right now that she wished to come in, for she would like to see how I dressed. I thought the request a strange one and brought the small person in to hear more of it. She told me,

"I heard my mamma and some other ladies talking about you," she said, "and wondering what you would be like; and they said that women like you who go out making speeches never know how to dress themselves, and they said that they bet a cent that you just flung your clothes on,— and do you? Because I think it must be lovely to be able to fling your clothes on—and I wish I could! Don't you tell that I told you, will you?—but that is why I came over. I live over there,"—she pointed to a house across the street,—"and I often come to this house. I brought over a jar of cream this morning. My mamma sent it over to Mrs. Price, because she was having you stay here."

"That was very kind of your mamma," I said, much pleased with this evidence of her mother's good-will.

"Oh, yes," said my visitor. "My mamma says she always likes to help people out when they are in trouble. But no one knows that I am here but just you and me. I watched and watched for you, and when you came nobody was looking and I slipped out and came right in, and never knocked—nor nothin'."

I assured my small guest that mum was the word, and that I should be delighted to have her for a spectator while I went on with the process of making myself look as nice as nature would allow. But she was plainly disappointed when she found that I was not one bit quicker about dressing than plenty of others, even though she tried to speed me up a little.

Soon the President came for me and took me to the Municipal Hall, where the meeting was to be held.

I knew, just as soon as I went in, that it was going to be a good meeting. There was a distinct air of preparedness about everything— some one had scrubbed the floor and put flags on the wall and flowers in the windows; over in the corner there was a long, narrow table piled up with cups and saucers, with cake and sandwiches carefully covered from sight; but I knew what caused the lumpiness under the white cloth. Womanly instinct—which has been declared a safer guide than man's reasoning—told me that there were going to be refreshments, and the

4

delightful odor of coffee, which escaped from the tightly closed boiler on the stove, confirmed my deductions. Then I noticed that a handbill on the wall spoke freely of it, and declared that every one was invited to stay, although there did not seem to be much need of this invitation—certainly there did not seem to be any climatic reason for any one's leaving any place of shelter; for now the wind, confirming our worst suspicions of it, began to drive frozen splinters of sleet against the windows.

By three o'clock the hall was full,—women mostly, for it was still the busy time for the men on the farms. Many of the women brought their children with them. Soon after I began to speak, the children fell asleep, tired out with struggling with wind and weather, and content to leave the affairs of state with any one who wanted them. But the women watched me with eager faces which seemed to speak back to me. The person who drives ten miles against a head wind over bad roads to hear a lecture is not generally disposed to slumber. The faces of these women were so bright and interested that, when it was over, it seemed to me that it had been a conversation where all had taken part.

The things that I said to them do not matter; they merely served as an introduction to what came after, when we sat around the stove and the young girls of the company brought us coffee and sandwiches, and mocha cake and home-made candy, and these women told me some of the things that are near their hearts.

"I drove fourteen miles to-day," said one woman, "but those of us who live long on the prairie do not mind these things. We were two hundred miles from a railway when we went in first, and we only got our mail 'in the spring.' Now, when we have a station within fourteen miles and a post-office on the next farm, we feel we are right in the midst of things, and I suppose we do not really mind the inconveniences that would seem dreadful to some people. We have done without things all our lives, always hoping for better things to come, and able to bear things that were disagreeable by telling ourselves that the children would have things easier than we had had them. We have had frozen crops; we have had hail; we have had serious sickness; but we have not complained, for all these things seemed to be God's doings, and no one could help it. We took all this—face upwards; but with the war—it is different. The war is not God's doings at all. Nearly all the boys from our neighborhood are gone, and some are not coming back——"

She stopped abruptly, and a silence fell on the group of us. She fumbled for a moment in her large black purse, and then handed me an envelope, worn, battered. It was addressed to a soldier in France and it had not been opened. Across the corner, in red ink, was written the words, "Killed in action."

5

"My letters are coming back now," she said simply. "Alex was my eldest boy, and he went at the first call for men, and he was only eighteen—he came through Saint-Éloi and Festubert—But this happened in September."

The woman who sat beside her took up the theme. "We have talked a lot about this at our Red Cross meetings. What do the women of the world think of war? No woman ever wanted war, did she? No woman could bring a child into the world, suffering for it, caring for it, loving it, without learning the value of human life, could she? War comes about because human life is the cheapest thing in the world; it has been taken at man's estimate, and that is entirely too low. Now, we have been wondering what can be done when this war is over to form a league of women to enforce peace. There is enough sentiment in the world in favor of human life if we could bind it up some way."

I gazed at the eager faces before me—in astonishment. Did I ever hear high-browed ladies in distant cities talk of the need of education in the country districts?

"Well-kept homes and hand-knit socks will never save the world," said Alex's mother. "Look at Germany! The German women are kind, patient, industrious, frugal, hard-working, everything that a woman ought to be, but it did not save them, or their country, and it will not save us. We have allowed men to have control of the big things in life too long. While we worked—or played—they have ruled. My nearest neighbor is a German, and she and I have talked these things over. She feels just the same as we do, and she sews for our Red Cross. She says she could not knit socks for our soldiers, for they are enemies, but she makes bandages, for she says wounded men are not enemies, and she is willing to do anything for them. She wanted to come to-day to hear you, but her husband would not let her have a horse, because he says he does not believe in women speaking in public, anyway! I wanted her to come with us even if he did not like it, but she said that she dared not."

"Were you not afraid of making trouble?" I asked.

Alex's mother smiled. "A quick, sharp fight is the best and clears up things. I would rather be a rebel any time than a slave. But of course it is easy for me to talk! I have always been treated like a human being. Perhaps it is just as well that she did not come. Old Hans has long generations back of him to confirm him in his theory that women are intended to be men's bondservants and that is why they are made smaller; it will all take time—and other things. The trouble has been with all of us that we have expected time to work out all of our difficulties, and it won't; there is no curative quality in time! And what I am most afraid of

6

is that we will settle down after the war, and slip right back into our old ways,—our old peaceful ways,—and let men go on ruling the world, and war will come again and again. Men have done their very best,—I am not feeling hard to them,—but I know, and the thoughtful men know, that men alone can never free the world from the blight of war; and if we go on, too gentle and sweet to assert ourselves, knitting, nursing, bringing children into the world, it will surely come to pass, when we are old, perhaps, and not able to do anything,—but suffer,—that war will come again, and we shall see our daughters' children or our granddaughters' children sent off to fight, and their heart-broken mothers will turn on us accusing eyes and say to us, 'You went through all this— you knew what this means—why didn't you do something?' That is my bad dream when I sit knitting, because I feel hard toward the women that are gone. They were a poor lot, many of them. I like now best of all Jennie Geddes who threw the stool at somebody's head. I forget what Jennie's grievance was, but it was the principle that counts—she had a conviction, and was willing to fight for it. I never said these things—until I got this." She still held the letter, with its red inscription, in her hand. "But now I feel that I have earned the right to speak out. I have made a heavy investment in the cause of Humanity and I am going to look after it. The only thing that makes it possible to give up Alex is the hope that Alex's death may help to make war impossible and so save other boys. But unless we do something his death will not help a bit; for this thing has always been—and that is the intolerable thought to me. I am willing to give my boy to die for others if I am sure that the others are going to be saved, but I am not willing that he should die in vain. You see what I mean, don't you?"

I told her that I did see, and that I believed that she had expressed the very thought that was in the mind of women everywhere.

"Well, then," she said quickly, "why don't you write it? We will forget this when it is all over and we will go back to our old pursuits and there will be nothing—I mean, no record of how we felt. Anyway, we will die and a new generation will take our places. Why don't you write it while your heart is hot?"

"But," I said, "perhaps what I should write would not truly represent what the women are thinking. They have diverse thoughts, and how can I hope to speak for them?"

"Write what you feel," she said sternly. "These are fundamental things. Ideas are epidemic—they go like the measles. If you are thinking a certain thing, you may be sure you have no monopoly of it; many others are thinking it too. That is my greatest comfort at this time. Write down what you feel, even if it is not what you think you ought to feel. Write it down for all of us!"

And that is how it happened. There in the Municipal Hall in the small town of Ripston, as we sat round the stove that cold November day, with the sleet sifting against the windows, I got my commission from these women, whom I had not seen until that day, to tell what we think and feel, to tell how it looks to us, who are the mothers of soldiers, and to whom even now the letter may be on its way with its curt inscription across the corner. I got my commission there to tell fearlessly and hopefully the story of the Next of Kin.

It will be written in many ways, by many people, for the brand of this war is not only on our foreheads, but deep in our hearts, and it will be reflected in all that our people write for many years to come. The trouble is that most of us feel too much to write well; for it is hard to write of the things which lie so heavy on our hearts; but the picture is not all dark— no picture can be. If it is all dark, it ceases to be a picture and becomes a blot. Belgium has its tradition of deathless glory, its imperishable memories of gallant bravery which lighten its darkness and make it shine like noonday. The one unlightened tragedy of the world to-day is Germany.

I thought of these things that night when I was being entertained at the Southern woman's hospitable home.

"It pretty near took a war to make these English women friendly to each other and to Americans. I lived here six months before any of them called on me, and then I had to go and dig them out; but I was not going to let them go on in such a mean way. They told me then that they were waiting to see what church I was going to; and then I rubbed it into them that they were a poor recommend for any church, with their mean, unneighborly ways; for if a church does not teach people to be friendly I think it ought to be burned down, don't you? I told them I could not take much stock in that hymn about 'We shall know each other there,' when they did not seem a bit anxious about knowing each other here, which is a heap more important; for in heaven we will all have angels to play with, but here we only have each other, and it is right lonesome when they won't come out and play! But I tell you things have changed for the better since the war, and now we knit and sew together, and forgive each other for being Methodists and Presbyterians; and, do you know? I made a speech one night, right out loud so everybody could hear me, in a Red Cross meeting, and that is what I thought that I could never do. But I got feeling so anxious about the prisoners of war in Germany that I couldn't help making an appeal for them; and I was so keen about it, and wanted every one of those dear boys to get a square meal, that I forgot all about

8

little Mrs. Price, and I was not caring a cent whether she was doing herself proud or not. And when I got done the people were using their handkerchiefs, and I was sniffing pretty hard myself, but we raised eighty-five dollars then and there, and now I know I will never be scared again. I used to think it was so ladylike to be nervous about speaking, and now I know it is just a form of selfishness. I was simply scared that I would not do well, thinking all the time of myself. But now everything has changed and I am ready to do anything I can."

"Go on," I said; "tell me some more. Remember that you women to-day made me promise to write down how this war is hitting us, and I merely promised to write what I heard and saw. I am not going to make up anything, so you are all under obligation to tell me all you can. I am not to be the author of this book, but only the historian."

"It won't be hard," she said encouragingly. "There is so much happening every day that it will be harder to decide what to leave out than to find things to put in. In this time of excitement the lid is off, I tell you; the bars are down; we can see right into the hearts of people. It is like a fire or an earthquake when all the doors are open and the folks are carrying their dearest possessions into the street, and they are all real people now, and they have lost all their little mincing airs and all their lawdie-daw. But believe me, we have been some fiddlers! When I look around this house I see evidence of it everywhere; look at that abomination now"—She pointed to an elaborately beaded match-safe which hung on the wall.

It bore on it the word, "Matches," in ornate letters, all made of beads, but I noticed that its empty condition belied the inscription.

"Think of the hours of labor that some one has put on that," she went on scornfully, "and now it is such an aristocrat that it takes up all its time at that and has no time to be useful. I know now that it never really intended to hold matches, but simply lives to mock the honest seeker who really needs a match. I have been a real sinner myself," she went on after a pause; "I have been a fiddler, all right. I may as well make a clean breast of it,—I made that match-safe and nearly bored my eyes out doing it, and was so nervous and cross that I was not fit to live with."

"I can't believe that," I said.

"Well, I sure was some snappy. I have teased out towel ends, and made patterns on them; I've punched holes in linen and sewed them up again— there is no form of foolishness that I have not committed—and liked it! But now I have ceased to be a fiddler and have become a citizen, and I am going to try to be a real good spoke in the wheel of progress. I can't express it very well, but I am going to try to link up with the people next

9

me and help them along. Perhaps you know what I mean—I think it is called team-play."

When the Parliament Buildings in Ottawa were burning, the main switch which controlled the lighting was turned off by mistake and the whole place was plunged into darkness, and this added greatly to the horror and danger. The switch was down a long passage through which the smoke was rolling, and it seemed impossible for any one to make the journey and return. Then the people who were there formed a chain, by holding each other's hands—a great human chain. So that the one who went ahead felt the sustaining power of the one who came behind him. If he stumbled and fell, the man behind him helped him to his feet and encouraged him to go on. In this way the switch was reached, the light was turned on, and many lives were saved.

Over the world to-day roll great billows of hatred and misunderstanding, which have darkened the whole face of the earth. We believe that there is a switch if we could get to it, but the smoke blinds us and we are choked with our tears. Perhaps if we join hands all of us will be able to do what a few of us could never do. This reaching-out of feeble human hands, this new compelling force which is going to bind us all together, this deep desire for cohesion which swells in our hearts and casts out all smallness and all self-seeking—this is what we mean when we speak of the Next of Kin. It is not a physical relationship, but the great spiritual bond which unites all those whose hearts have grown more tender by sorrow, and whose spiritual eyes are not dimmed, but washed clearer by their tears!

Sing a song of hearts grown tender, With the sorrow and the pain; Sorrow is a great old mender, Love can give,—and give again. Love's a prodigal old spender,— And the jolliest old lender, For he never turns away Any one who comes to borrow, If they say their stock is slender, And they're sorely pressed by sorrow! Never has been known to say,— "We are short ourselves to-day,— Can't you come again to-morrow?" That has never been Love's way! And he's rich beyond all telling, Love divine all love excelling!

CHAPTER I
BEACH DAYS

When a soldier's watch, with its luminous face, Loses its light and grows dim and black, He holds it out in the sun a space And the radiance all comes back; And that is the reason I'm thinking to-day Of the glad days now long past; I am leaving my heart where the sunbeams play: I am trying to drive my fears away: I am charging my soul with a spirit gay, And hoping that it will last!

We were the usual beach crowd, with our sport suits, our silk sweaters, our Panama hats, our veranda teas and week-end guests, our long, lovely, lazy afternoons in hammocks beside the placid waters of Lake Winnipeg. Life was easy and pleasant, as we told ourselves life ought to be in July and August, when people work hard all year and then come away to the quiet greenness of the big woods, to forget the noise and dust of the big city.

We called our cottage "Kee-am," for that is the Cree word which means "Never mind"—"Forget it"—"I should worry!" and we liked the name. It had a romantic sound, redolent of the old days when the Indians roamed through these leafy aisles of the forest, and it seemed more fitting and dignified than "Rough House," where dwelt the quietest family on the beach, or "Dunwurkin" or "Neverdunfillin" or "Takitezi," or any of the other more or less home-made names. We liked our name so well that we made it, out of peeled poles, in wonderful rustic letters, and put it up in the trees next the road.

Looking back now, we wonder what we had to worry about! There was politics, of course; we had just had a campaign that warmed up our little province, and some of the beachites were not yet speaking to each other; but nobody had been hurt and nobody was in jail.

Religion was not troubling us: we went dutifully every Sunday to the green-and-white schoolhouse under the tall spruce trees, and heard a sermon preached by a young man from the college, who had a deep and intimate knowledge of Amos and Elisha and other great men long dead, and sometimes we wished he would tell us more about the people who are living now and leave the dead ones alone. But it is always safer to speak of things that have happened long ago, and aspersions may be cast with impunity on Ahab and Jezebel and Balak. There is no danger that they will have friends on the front seat, who will stop their subscriptions to the building fund because they do not believe in having politics introduced into the church.

The congregations were small, particularly on the hot afternoons, for many of our people did not believe in going to church when the weather was not just right. Indeed, there had been a serious discussion in the synod of one of the largest churches on the question of abolishing prayers altogether in the hot weather; and I think that some one gave notice of a motion that would come up to this effect at the annual meeting. No; religion was not a live topic. There were evidently many who had said, as did one little girl who was leaving for her holidays, "Good-bye, God—we are going to the country."

One day a storm of excitement broke over us, and for a whole afternoon upset the calm of our existence. Four hardy woodmen came down the road with bright new axes, and began to cut down the beautiful trees which had taken so many years to grow and which made one of the greatest beauties of the beach. It was some minutes before the women sitting on their verandas realized what was happening; but no army ever mobilized quicker for home defense than they, and they came in droves demanding an explanation, of which there did not seem to be any.

"Big Boss him say cut down tree," the spokesman of the party said over and over again.

The women in plain and simple language expressed their unexpurgated opinion of Big Boss, and demanded that he be brought to them. The stolid Mikes and Peters were utterly at a loss to know what to do!

"Big Boss—no sense," one woman roared at them, hoping to supplement their scanty knowledge of English with volume of sound.

There was no mistaking what the gestures meant, and at last the wood-choppers prepared to depart, the smallest man of the party muttering something under his breath which sounded like an anti-suffrage speech. I think it was, "Woman's place is the home," or rather its Bukawinian equivalent. We heard nothing further from them, and indeed we thought no more of it, for the next day was August 4, 1914.

When the news of war came, we did not really believe it! War! That was over! There had been war, of course, but that had been long ago, in the dark ages, before the days of free schools and peace conferences and missionary conventions and labor unions! There might be a little fuss in Ireland once in a while. The Irish are privileged, and nobody should begrudge them a little liberty in this. But a big war—that was quite impossible! Christian nations could not go to war!

"Somebody should be made to pay dear for this," tearfully declared a doctor's wife. "This is very bad for nervous women."

12

The first news had come on the 9.40 train, and there was no more until the 6.20 train when the men came down from the city; but they could throw no light on it either. The only serious face that I saw was that of our French neighbor, who hurried away from the station without speaking to any one. When I spoke to him the next day, he answered me in French, and I knew his thoughts were far away.

The days that followed were days of anxious questioning. The men brought back stories of the great crowds that surged through the streets blocking the traffic in front of the newspaper offices reading the bulletins, while the bands played patriotic airs; of the misguided German who shouted, "Hoch der Kaiser!" and narrowly escaped the fury of the crowd.

We held a monster meeting one night at "Windwhistle Cottage," and we all made speeches, although none of us knew what to say. The general tone of the speeches was to hold steady,—not to be panicky,—Britannia rules the waves,—it would all be over soon,—Dr. Robertson Nicholl and Kitchener could settle anything!

The crowd around the dancing pavilion began to dwindle in the evenings—that is, of the older people. The children still danced, happily; fluffy-haired little girls, with "headache" bands around their pretty heads, did the fox-trot and the one-step with boys of their own age and older, but the older people talked together in excited groups.

Every night when the train came in the crowds waited in tense anxiety to get the papers, and when they were handed out, read them in silence, a silence which was ominous. Political news was relegated to the third page and was not read until we got back to the veranda. In these days nothing mattered; the baker came late; the breakfast dishes were not washed sometimes until they were needed for lunch, for the German maids and the English maids discussed the situation out under the trees. Mary, whose last name sounded like a tray of dishes falling, the fine-looking Polish woman who brought us vegetables every morning, arrived late and in tears, for she said, "This would be bad times for Poland—always it was bad times for Poland, and I will never see my mother again."

A shadow had fallen on us, a shadow that darkened the children's play. Now they made forts of sand, and bored holes in the ends of stove-wood to represent gaping cannon's mouths, and played that half the company were Germans; but before many days that game languished, for there were none who would take the German part: every boat that was built now was a battleship, and every kite was an aeroplane and loaded with bombs!

13

In less than a week we were collecting for a hospital ship to be the gift of Canadian women. The message was read out in church one afternoon, and volunteer collectors were asked for. So successful were these collectors all over Canada that in a few days word came to us that enough money had been raised, and that all moneys collected then could be given to the Belgian Relief Fund. The money had simply poured in— it was a relief to give!

Before the time came for school to begin, there were many closed cottages, for the happy careless freedom of the beach was gone; there is no happiness in floating across a placid lake in a flat-bottomed boat if you find yourself continually turning your head toward the shore, thinking that you hear some one shouting, "Extra."

There were many things that made it hard to leave the place where we had spent so many happy hours. There was the rustic seat we had made ourselves, which faced the lake, and on which we had sat and seen the storms gather on Blueberry Island. It was a comfortable seat with the right slant in its back, and I am still proud of having helped to make it. There was the breakwater of logs which were placed with such feats of strength, to prevent the erosion of the waves, and which withstood the big storm of September, 1912, when so many breakwaters were smashed to kindling-wood. We always had intended to make a long box along the top, to plant red geraniums in, but it had not been done. There was the dressing-tent where the boys ran after their numerous swims, and which had been the scene of many noisy quarrels over lost garments—garters generally, for they have an elusive quality all their own. There was also the black-poplar stump which a misguided relative of mine said "no woman could split." He made this remark after I had tried in vain to show him what was wrong with his method of attack. I said that I thought he would do better if he could manage to hit twice in the same place! And he said that he would like to see me do it, and went on to declare that he would bet me a five-dollar bill that I could not.

If it were not for the fatal curse of modesty I would tell how eagerly I grasped the axe and with what ease I hit, not twice, but half a dozen times in the same place—until the stump yielded. This victory was all the sweeter to me because it came right after our sports day when I had entered every available contest, from the nail-driving competition to the fat woman's race, and had never even been mentioned as among those present!

We closed our cottage on August 24. That day all nature conspired to make us feel sorry that we were leaving. A gentle breeze blew over the lake and rasped its surface into dancing ripples that glittered in the sun. Blueberry Island seemed to stand out clear and bold and beckoning.

14

White-winged boats lay over against the horizon and the *chug-chug* of a motor-boat came at intervals in a lull of the breeze. The more tender varieties of the trees had begun to show a trace of autumn coloring, just a hint and a promise of the ripened beauty of the fall—if we would only stay!

Before the turn in the road hid it from sight we stopped and looked back at the "Kee-am Cottage"—my last recollection of it is of the boarded windows, which gave it the blinded look of a dead thing, and of the ferns which grandma had brought from the big woods beyond the railway track and planted all round it, and which had grown so quickly and so rank that they seemed to fill in all the space under the cottage, and with their pale-green, feathery fringe, to be trying to lift it up into the sunshine above the trees. Instinctively we felt that we had come to the end of a very pleasant chapter in our life as a family; something had disturbed the peaceful quiet of our lives; somewhere a drum was beating and a fife was calling!

Not a word of this was spoken, but Jack suddenly put it all into words, for he turned to me and asked quickly, "Mother, when will I be eighteen?"

Gay, as the skater who blithely whirls To the place of the dangerous ice! Content, as the lamb who nibbles the grass While the butcher sets the price! So content and gay were the boys at play In the nations near and far, When munition kings and diplomats Cried, "War! War!! War!!!"

CHAPTER II
WORKING IN!

The day after we went to the city I got my first real glimpse of war! It was the white face of our French neighbor. His wife and two little girls had gone to France a month before the war broke out, and were visiting his family in a village on the Marne. Since the outbreak of war he had had no word from them, and his face worked pitifully when he told me

15

this. "Not one word, though I cabled and got friends in London to wire *aussi*," he said. "But I will go myself and see."

"What about your house and motor?" he was asked.

He raised his shoulders and flung out his hands. "What difference?" he said; "I will not need them."

I saw him again the day he left. He came out of his house with a small Airedale pup which had been the merry playmate of Alette and Yvonne. He stood on the veranda holding the dog in his arms. Strangers were moving into the house and their boxes stood on the floor. I went over to say good-bye.

"I will not come back," he said simply; "it will be a long fight; we knew it would come, but we did not know when. If I can but find wife and children—but the Germans—they are devils—Boches—no one knows them as we do!"

He stood irresolute a moment, then handed me the dog and went quickly down the steps.

"It is for France!" he said.

I sat on the veranda railing and watched him go. The Airedale blinded his eyes looking after him, then looked at me, plainly asking for an explanation. But I had to tell him that I knew no more about it than he did. Then I tried to comfort him by telling him that many little dogs were much worse off than he, for they had lost their people and their good homes as well, and he still had his comfortable home and his good meals. But it was neither meals nor bed that his faithful little heart craved, and for many weeks a lonely little Airedale on Chestnut Street searched diligently for his merry little playmates and his kind master, but he found them not.

There was still a certain unreality about it all. Sometimes it has been said that the men who went first went for adventure. Perhaps they did, but it does not matter—they have since proved of what sort of stuff they were made.

When one of the first troop trains left Winnipeg, a handsome young giant belonging to the Seventy-ninth Highlanders said, as he swung himself up on the rear coach, "The only thing I am afraid of is that it will all be over before we get there." He was needlessly alarmed, poor lad! He was in time for everything; Festubert, Saint-Éloi, Ypres; for the gas attacks before the days of gas-masks, for trench-fever, for the D.C.M.; and now, with but one leg, and blind, he is one of the happy warriors at St. Dunstan's whose cheerfulness puts to shame those of us who are whole!

There were strange scenes at the station when those first trains went out. The Canadians went out with a flourish, with cheers, with songs, with rousing music from the bands. The serious men were the French and Belgian reservists, who, silently, carrying their bundles, passed through our city, with grim, determined faces. They knew, and our boys did not know, to what they were going. That is what made the difference in their manner.

The government of one of the provinces, in the early days of the war, shut down the public works, and, strange to say, left the bars open. Their impulse was right—but they shut down the wrong thing; it should have been the bars, of course. They knew something should be shut down. We are not blaming them; it was a panicky time. People often, when they hear the honk of an automobile horn, jump back instead of forward. And it all came right in time.

A moratorium was declared at once, which for the time being relieved people of their debts, for there was a strong feeling that the cup of sorrow was so full now that all movable trouble should be set off for another day!

The temperance people then asked, as a corresponding war measure, that the bars be closed. They urged that the hearts of our people were already so burdened that they should be relieved of the trouble and sorrow which the liquor traffic inevitably brings. "Perhaps," they said to the government, "when a happier season comes, we may be able to bear it better; but we have so many worries now, relieve us of this one, over which you have control."

Then the financial side of the liquor traffic began to pinch. Manitoba was spending thirteen million dollars over the bars every year. The whole Dominion's drink bill was one hundred millions. When the people began to rake and save to meet the patriotic needs, and to relieve the stress of unemployment, these great sums of money were thought of longingly— and with the longing which is akin to pain! The problem of unemployment was aggravated by the liquor evil and gave another argument for prohibition.

I heard a woman telling her troubles to a sympathetic friend one day, as we rode in an elevator.

"'E's all right when 'e's in work," she said; "but when 'e's hidle 'e's something fierce: 'e knocks me about crool. 'E guzzles all the time 'e's out of work."

It was easy to believe. Her face matched her story; she was a poor, miserable, bedraggled creature, with teeth out in front. She wore black cotton gloves such as undertakers supply for the pallbearers, and every finger was out. The liquor traffic would have a better chance if there were not so many arguments against it walking round.

About this time, too, the traffic suffered a great bereavement, for the personal liberty argument fell, mortally wounded. The war did that, too.

All down the ages there have been men who believed that personal liberty included the right to do what one wished to do, no matter who was hurt. So, if a man wished to drink, by the sacred rights for which his forefathers had bled and died he was at liberty to do so, and then go home and beat up his own wife and family if he wanted to; for if you can't beat your own wife, whom can you beat, I'd like to know? Any one who disputed this sacred right was counted a spoil-fun and a joy-killer!

But a change came over the world's thought in the early days of the war. Liberty grew to be a holy word, a sacred thing, when the blood of our brightest and best was being poured out in its defense, and never again will the old, selfish, miserable conception of liberty obtain favor. The Kaiser helped here, too, for he is such a striking example of the one who claims absolute liberty for himself, no matter who is hurt, that somehow we never hear it mentioned now. I believe it is gone, forever!

The first step in the curtailment of the liquor traffic was the closing of the bars at seven o'clock, and the beneficial effect was felt at once. Many a man got home early for the first time in his life, and took his whole family to the "movies."

The economy meetings brought out some quaint speeches. No wonder! People were taken unawares. We were unprepared for war, and the changes it had brought;—we were as unprepared as the woman who said, in speaking of unexpected callers, "I had not even time to turn my plants." There was much unintentional humor. One lady, whose home was one of the most beautiful in the city, and who entertained lavishly, told us, in her address on "Economy," that at the very outbreak of the war she reduced her cook's wages from thirty to twenty dollars, and gave the difference to the Patriotic Fund; that she had found a cheaper dressmaker who made her dresses now for fifteen dollars, where formerly she had paid twenty-five; and she added artlessly, "They are really nicer, and I do think we should all give in these practical ways; that's the sort of giving that I really enjoy!"

Another woman told of how much she had given up for the Patriotic Fund; that she had determined not to give one Christmas present, and had given up all the societies to which she had belonged, even the Missionary Society, and was giving it all to the Red Cross. "I will not even give a present to the boy who brings the paper," she declared with conviction. Whether or not the boy's present ever reached the Red Cross, I do not know. But ninety-five per cent of the giving was real, honest, hard, sacrificing giving. Elevator-boys, maids, stenographers gave a percentage of their earnings, and gave it joyously. They like to give, but they do not like to have it taken away from them by an employer, who thereby gets the credit of the gift. The Red Cross mite-boxes into which children put their candy money, while not enriching the Red Cross to any large extent, trained the children to take some share in the responsibility; and one enthusiastic young citizen, who had been operated on for appendicitis, proudly exhibited his separated appendix, preserved in alcohol, at so much per look, and presented the proceeds to the Red Cross.

The war came home to the finest of our people first. It has not reached them all yet, but it is working in, like the frost into the cellars when the thermometer shows forty degrees below zero. Many a cellar can stand a week of this—but look out for the second! Every day it comes to some one.

"I don't see why we are always asked to give," one woman said gloomily, when the collector asked her for a monthly subscription to the Red Cross. "Every letter that goes out of the house has a stamp on it— and we write a queer old lot of letters, and I guess we've done our share."

She is not a dull woman either or hard of heart. It has not got to her yet—that's all! I cannot be hard on her in my judgment, for it did not come to me all at once, either.

When I saw the first troops going away, I wondered how their mothers let them go, and I made up my mind that I would not let my boy go,—I was so glad he was only seventeen,—for hope was strong in our hearts that it might be over before he was of military age. It was the Lusitania that brought me to see the whole truth. Then I saw that we were waging war on the very Princes of Darkness, and I knew that morning when I read the papers, I knew that it would be better—a thousand times better—to be dead than to live under the rule of people whose hearts are so utterly black and whose process of reasoning is so oxlike—they are so stupidly brutal. I knew then that no man could die better than in defending civilization from this ghastly thing which threatened her!

Soon after that I knew, without a word being said, that my boy wanted to go—I saw the seriousness come into his face, and knew what it meant. It was when the news from the Dardanelles was heavy on our hearts, and the newspapers spoke gravely of the outlook.

One day he looked up quickly and said, "I want to go—I want to help the British Empire—while there is a British Empire!"

19

And then I realized that my boy, my boy, had suddenly become a man and had put away childish things forever.

I shall always be glad that the call came to him, not in the intoxication of victory, but in the dark hour of apparent defeat.

CHAPTER III
LET'S PRETEND

Let's pretend the skies are blue, Let's pretend the world is new, And the birds of hope are singing All the day!

Short of gladness—learn to fake it! Long on sadness—go and shake it! Life is only—what you make it, Anyway!

There is wisdom without end In the game of "Let's pretend!"

We played it to-day. We had to, for the boys went away, and we had to send our boys away with a smile! They will have heartaches and homesickness a-plenty, without going away with their memories charged with a picture of their mothers in tears, for that's what takes the heart out of a boy. They are so young, so brave, we felt that we must not fail them.

With such strong words as these did we admonish each other, when we met the last night, four of us, whose sons were among the boys who were going away. We talked hard and strong on this theme, not having a very good grip on it ourselves, I am afraid. We simply harangued each other on the idleness of tears at stations. Every one of us had something to say; and when we parted, it was with the tacit understanding that there was an Anti-Tear League formed—the boys were leaving on an early train in the morning!

The morning is a dismal time anyway, and teeth will chatter, no matter how brave you feel! It is a squeamish, sickly, choky time,—a winter morning before the sun is up; and you simply cannot eat breakfast when you look round the table and see every chair filled,—even the five-year-old fellow is on hand,—and know that a long, weary time is ahead of the

20

one who sits next you before he comes again to his father's house. Even though the conversation is of the gayest, every one knows what every one else is thinking.

***

There is no use trying—I cannot write the story of that morning.... I will tell you of other troop-trains I have seen go. I will tell you of another boy who carried off all the good-byes with a high hand and great spirits, and said something to every one of the girls who brought him candy, telling one that he would remember her in his will, promising another that he would marry her when he got to be Admiral of the Swiss Navy, but who, when he came to say good-bye to his father, suddenly grew very white and very limp, and could only say, "Oh, dad! Good old dad!"

***

I will tell you of other troop-trains I have seen go out, with other boys waving to other women who strained their eyes and winked hard, hard, hard to keep back the tears, and stood still, quite still until the last car had disappeared around the bend, and the last whistle had torn the morning air into shreds and let loose a whole wild chorus of echoes through the quiet streets!

***

There was a mist in the air this morning, and a white frost covered the trees with beautiful white crystals that softened their leafless limbs. It made a soft and graceful drapery on the telegraph poles and wires. It carpeted the edges of the platform that had not been walked on, and even covered the black roofs of the station buildings and the flatcars which stood in the yard. It seemed like a beautiful white decoration for the occasion, a beautiful, heavy, elaborate mourning—for those who had gone—and white, of course—all white,—because they were so young!

***

Then we came home. It was near the opening time of the stores, and the girls were on their way to work, but their footfalls made no sound on the pavement. Even the street-cars seemed to glide quietly by. The city seemed grave and serious and sad, and disposed to go softly.... In the store windows the blinds were still down—ghastly, shirred white things which reminded me uncomfortably of the lining of a coffin! Over the hotel on the corner, the Calgary Beer Man, growing pale in the sickly dawn, still poured—and lifted—and drank—and poured—and lifted—and drank,—insatiable as the gods of war.

***

21

I wandered idly through the house—what a desolate thing a house can be when every corner of it holds a memory!—not a memory either, for that bears the thought of something past,—when every corner of it is full of a boyish presence!... I can hear him rushing down the stairs in the morning to get the paper, and shouting the headlines to me as he brings it up. I can hear him come in at the front door and thump his books down on the hall seat, and call "Mother!" I sit down and summon them all, for I know they will fade soon enough—the thin, sharp edge of everything wears mercifully blunt in time!

Then I gathered up his schoolbooks, and every dog-eared exercise-book, and his timetable, which I found pinned on his window curtain, and I carried them up to the storeroom in the attic, with his baseball mitt—and then, for the first time, as I made a pile of the books under the beams, I broke my anti-tear pledge. It was not for myself, or for my neighbor across the street whose only son had gone, or for the other mothers who were doing the same things all over the world; it was not for the young soldiers who had gone out that day; it was for the boys who had been cheated of their boyhood, and who had to assume men's burdens, although in years they were but children. The saddest places of all the world to-day are not the battle fields, or the hospitals, or the cross-marked hillsides where the brave ones are buried; the saddest places are the deserted campus and playgrounds where they should be playing; the empty seats in colleges, where they should be sitting; the spaces in the ranks of happy, boisterous schoolboys, from which the brave boys have gone,—these boys whose boyhood has been cut so pitifully short. I thought, too, of the little girls whose laughter will ring out no more in the careless, happy abandonment of girlhood, for the black shadow of anxiety and dread has fallen even on their young hearts; the tiny children, who, young as they are, know that some great sorrow has come to every one; the children of the war countries, with their terror-stricken eyes and pale faces; the unspeakable, unforgivable wrong that has been done to youth the world over.

There, as I sat on the floor of the storeroom, my soul wandered down a long, dark, silent valley, and met the souls of the mothers of all countries, who had come there, like me, to mourn ... and our tears were very hot, and very bitter ... for we knew that it was the Valley of Lost Childhood!

CHAPTER IV
PICTURES

Nothing is lost that our memories hold, Nothing forgotten that once we knew; And to-day a boy with curls of gold Is running my fond heart through and through— In and out and round and round— And I find myself laughing without a sound At the funny things he said that time When life was one glad nursery rhyme.

It should not be so hard for mothers to give up their children. We should grow accustomed to it, for we are always losing them. I once had a curly-haired baby with eyes like blue forget-me-nots, who had a sweet way of saying his words, and who coined many phrases which are still in use in my family. Who is there who cannot see that "a-ging-a-wah" has a much more refreshing sound than "a drink of water"? And I am sure that nobody could think of a nicer name for the hammer and nails than a "num and a peedaw." At an incredibly early age this baby could tell you how the birdies fly and what the kitty says.

All mothers who have had really wonderful children—and this takes us all in—will understand how hard it is to set these things down in cold print or even to tell them; for even our best friends are sometimes dull of heart and slow of understanding when we tell them perfectly wonderful things that our children did or said. We all know that horrible moment of suspense when we have told something real funny that our baby said, and our friends look at us with a dull is-that-all expression in their faces, and we are forced to supplement our recital by saying that it was not so much what he said as the way he said it!

Soon I lost the blue-eyed baby, and there came in his place a sturdy little freckle-faced chap, with a distinct dislike for water as a cleansing agent, who stoutly declared that washing his hands was a great waste of time, for they were sure to get dirty again; which seems to be reasonable, and it is a wonder that people have not taken this fact into account more when dealing with the griminess of youth. Who objected to going to church twice a day on the ground that he "might get too fond of it." Who, having once received five cents as recompense for finding his wayward sister, who had a certain proclivity for getting lost, afterwards deliberately mislaid the same sister and claimed the usual rates for finding her, and in this manner did a thriving "Lost and Found" business for days, until his unsuspecting parent overheard him giving his sister full directions for losing herself—he had grown tired of having to go with her each time, and claimed that as she always got half of the treat she should do her share of the work. Who once thrashed a boy who said that his sister had a dirty face,—which was quite true, but people do not need to say everything they know, do they? Who went swimming in the gravel pit long before the 24th of May, which marks the beginning of swimming and barefoot time in all proper families, and would have got away with it, too, only, in his haste to get a ride home, he and his friend changed shirts by mistake, and it all came to light at bedtime.

Then I lost him, too. There came in his place a tall youth with a distinct fondness for fine clothes, stiff collars, tan boots, and bright ties; a dignified young man who was pained and shocked at the disreputable appearance of a younger brother who was at that time passing through the wash-never period of his life and who insisted upon claiming relationship even in public places. Who hung his room with flags and pennants and photographs. Who had for his friends many young fellows with high pompadours, whom he called by their surnames and disputed with noisily and abusively, but, unlike the famous quarrel of Fox and Burke, "with no loss of friendship." Who went in his holidays as "mule-skinner" on a construction gang in the North Country, and helped to build the railway into "The Crossing," and came home all brown and tanned, with muscles as hard as iron and a luscious growth of whiskers. Who then went back to college and really began to work, for he had learned a few things about the value of an education as he drove the mules over the dump, which can be learned only when the muscles ache and the hands have blisters.

Then came the call! And again I lost him! But there is a private in the "Princess Pats" who carries my picture in his cap and who reads my letter over again just before "going in."

CHAPTER V

SAVING OUR SOULS

O work—thrice blessed of the gods— Abundant may you be! To hold us steady, when our hearts Grow cold and panicky!

I cannot fret—and drive the plough,— Nor weep—and ply the spade; O blessed work—I need you now To keep me unafraid!

No terrors can invade the place Where honest green things thrive; Come blisters—backache—sunburnt face— And save my soul alive!

No wonder that increased production has become a popular cry. Every one wants to work in a garden—a garden is so comforting and reassuring. Everything else has changed, but seedtime and harvest still remain. Rain still falls, seeds sprout, buds break into leaves, and blossoms are replaced by fruit.

We are forced back to the elemental things. Horses and cattle look better to me every day. Read the war news—which to-day tells of the destruction of French villages—and then look at the cattle grazing peacefully on the grass which clothes the hillside, and see how good they look! They look like sanctified Christians to me!

Ever since the war I have envied them. They are not suspicious or jealous; they are not worried, hurried, troubled, or afraid; they are oblivious of public opinion; they have no debts to pay; they do not weary you with explanations; they are not sorry for anything they have ever done; they are not blaming God for anything! On every count the cattle seem to have the best of us!

It is a quiet evening here in northern Alberta, and the evening light is glinting on the frozen ponds. I can see far up the valley as I write, and one by one the lights begin to glimmer in the farmhouses; and I like to think that supper is being prepared there for hungry children. The thought of supper appeals to me because there is no dining-car on the train, and every minute I am growing hungrier. The western sky burns red with the sunset, and throws a sullen glow on the banks of clouds in the east. It is a quiet, peaceful evening, and I find it hard to believe that somewhere men are killing each other and whole villages are burning.... The light on the ponds grows dimmer, with less of rose and more of a luminous gray.... I grow hungrier still, and I know it is just because I cannot get anything. I eat apples and nut-bars, but they do not satisfy me; it is roast beef, brown gravy, potatoes, and turnips that I want. Is it possible that I refused lemon pie—last night—at Carmangay? Well— well—let this be a lesson to you!

The sunset is gone now, and there is only a brightness in the western sky, and a big staring moon stands above the valley, shining down on the patches of snow which seem to run together like the wolves we used to see on the prairies of Manitoba long ago. The farmhouses we pass are bright with lights, and I know the children are gathered around the table to "do" their lessons. The North Country, with its long, snowy winters, develops the love of home in the hearts of our people, and drives the children indoors to find their comfort around the fire. Solomon knew this when he said that the perfect woman "is not afraid of the snow for her household." Indeed, no; she knows that the snow is a home-developing agency, and that no one knows the joy and comfort of home like those of us who have battled with cold and storm and drifted roads all day, and at nightfall come safely to this blessed place where warmth and companionship await us! Life has its compensations.

Across the aisle from me two women are knitting—not in a neighborly, gossipy way, chatting meanwhile, but silently, swiftly, nervously. There is a psychological reason for women knitting just now, beyond the need of socks. I know how these women feel! I, even I, have begun to crochet! I do it for the same reason that the old toper in time of stress takes to his glass. It keeps me from thinking; it atrophies the brain; and now I know why the women of the East are so slow about getting the franchise. They crochet and work in wool instead of thinking. You can't do both! When the casualty lists are long, and letters from the Front far apart—I crochet.

Once, when I was in great pain, the doctor gave me chloroform, and it seemed to me that a great black wall arose between me and pain! The pain was there all right, but it could not get to me on account of the friendly wall which held it back—and I was grateful! Now I am grateful to have a crochet-needle and a ball of silcotton. It is a sort of mental chloroform. This is for the real dark moments, when the waves go over our heads.... We all have them, but of course they do not last.

More and more am I impressed with the wonderful comeback of the human soul. We are like those Chinese toys, which, no matter how they are buffeted, will come back to an upright position. It takes a little longer with us—that is all; but given half a chance—or less—people will rise victorious over sin and sorrow, defeat and failure, and prove thereby the divinity which is in all of us!

As the light dimmed outside, I had time to observe my two traveling companions more closely. Though at first sight they came under the same general description of "middle-aged women, possibly grandmothers, industriously knitting," there was a wide difference between them as I observed them further. One had a face which bore traces of many disappointments, and had now settled down into a state of

26

sadness that was hopeless and final. She had been a fine-looking woman once, too, and from her high forehead and well-shaped mouth I should take her to be a woman of considerable mental power, but there had been too much sorrow; she had belonged to a house of too much trouble, and it had dried up the fountains of her heart. I could only describe her by one word, "winter-killed"! She was like a tree which had burst into bud at the coaxing of the soft spring zephyrs again and again, only to be caught each time by the frost, and at last, when spring really came, it could win no answering thrill, for the heart of the tree was "winter-killed." The frost had come too often!

The other woman was older, more wrinkled, more weather-beaten, but there was a childlike eagerness about her that greatly attracted me. She used her hands when she spoke, and smiled often. This childish enthusiasm contrasted strangely with her old face, and seemed like the spirit of youth fluttering still around the grave of one whom it loved!

I soon found myself talking to them; the old lady was glad to talk to me, for she was not making much headway with her companion, on whom all her arguments were beating in vain.

"I tell her she has no call to be feeling so bad about the war!" she began, getting right into the heart of the subject; "we didn't start it! Let the Kings and Kaisers and Czars who make the trouble do the fretting. Thank God, none of them are any blood-relation of mine, anyway. I won't fret over any one's sins, only my own, and maybe I don't fret half enough over them, either!"

"What do you know about sins?" the other woman said; "you couldn't sin if you tried——"

"That's all you know about it," said the old lady with what was intended for a dark and mysterious look; "but I never could see what good it does to worry, anyway, and bother other people by feeling sorry. Now, here she is worrying night and day because her boy is in the army and will have to go to France pretty soon. She has two others at home, too young to go. Harry is still safe in England—he may never have to go: the war may be over—the Kaiser may fall and break his neck—there's lots of ways peace may come. Even if Harry does go, he may not get killed. He may only get his toe off, or his little finger, and come home, or he may escape everything. Some do. Even if he is killed—every one has to die, and no one can die a better way; and Harry is ready—good and ready! So why does she fret? I know she's had trouble—lots of it—Lord, haven't we all? My three boys went—two have been killed; but I am not complaining—I am still hoping the last boy may come through safe.

27

Anyway, we couldn't help it. It is not our fault; we have to keep on doing what we can....

"I remember a hen I used to have when we lived on the farm, and she had more sense than lots of people—she was a little no-breed hen, and so small that nobody ever paid much attention to her. But she had a big heart, and was the greatest mother of any hen I had, and stayed with her chickens until they were as big as she was and refused to be gathered under wings any longer. She never could see that they were grown up. One time she adopted a whole family that belonged to a stuck-up Plymouth Rock that deserted them when they weren't much more than feathered. Biddy stepped right in and raised them, with thirteen of her own. Hers were well grown—Biddy always got down to business early in the spring, she was so forehanded. She raised the Plymouth Rocks fine, too! She was a born stepmother. Well, she got shut out one night, and froze her feet, and lost some good claws, too; but I knew she'd manage some way, and of course I did not let her set, because she could not scratch with these stumpy feet of hers. But she found a job all right! She stole chickens from the other hens. I often wondered what she promised them, but she got them someway, and only took those that were big enough to scratch, for Biddy knew her limitations. She was leading around twenty-two chickens of different sizes that summer.

"You see she had personality—that hen: you couldn't keep her down; she never went in when it rained, and she could cackle louder than any hen on the ground; and above all, she took things as they came. I always admired her. I liked the way she died, too. Of course I let her live as long as she could—she wouldn't have been any good to eat, anyway, for she was all brains, and I never could bear to make soup out of a philosopher like what she was. Well, she was getting pretty stiff—I could see that; and sometimes she had to try two or three times before she could get on the roost. But this night she made it on the first try, and when I went to shut the door, she sat there all ruffled up. I reached out to feel her, she looked so humped-up, and the minute I touched her, she fell off the roost; and when I picked her up, she was dead! You see, she got herself balanced so she would stay on the roost, and then died—bluffed it out to the last, and died standing up! That's what we should all try to do!" she concluded; "go down with a smile—I say—hustling and cheerful to the last!"

I commended her philosophy, but the other woman sat silent, and her knitting lay idle on her knee.

After all, the biggest thing in life is the mental attitude!

This was the third time a boy on a wheel Had come to her gate With the small yellow slip, with its few curt words, To tell her the fate Of the boys she had given to fight For the right to be free! I thought I must go as a neighbor and friend And stand by her side; At least I could tell her how sorry I was That a brave man had died.

She sat in a chair when I entered the room, With the thing in her hand, And the look on her face had a light and a bloom I could not understand. Then she showed me the message and said, With a sigh of respite,— "My last boy is dead. I can sleep. I can sleep Without dreaming to-night."

CHAPTER VI
SURPRISES

When all the evidence is in— When all the good—and all the sin— The Impulses—without—within Are catalogued—with reasons showing— What great surprises will await The small, the near-great and the great Who thought they knew how things were going!

Stories crowd in upon me as I write. Let no one ever say that this is a dull world! It is anything but dull! It is a pitiful, heartbreaking world, full of injustice, misunderstandings, false standards, and selfishness, but it is never dull. Neither is it a lost world, for the darkest corners of it are illuminated here and there by heroic deeds and noble aspirations. Men who hilariously sold their vote and influence prior to 1914, who took every sharp turn within the law, and who shamelessly mocked at any ideals of citizenship, were among the first to put on the King's uniform and march out to die.

To-day I read in the "paper from home" that Private William Keel is "missing, believed killed"; and it took me back to the old days before the war when the late Private Keel was accustomed to hold up the little town. Mr. Keel was a sober man—except upon occasions. The occasions were not numerous, but they left an undying impression on his neighbors and fellow townsmen; for the late private had a way all his own. He was a big

Welshman, so strong that he never knew how strong he was; and when he became obsessed with the desire to get drunk, no one could stop him. He had to have it out. At such times his one ambition was to ride a horse up the steps of the hotel, and then—George Washington-like—rise in his stirrups and deliver an impassioned address on what we owe to the Old Flag. If he were blocked or thwarted in this, he became dangerous and hard to manage, and sometimes it took a dozen men to remove him to the Police Station. When he found himself safely landed there, with a locked door and small, barred window between himself and liberty, his mood changed and the remainder of the night was spent in song, mostly of "A life on the ocean wave and a home on the rolling deep"; for he had been a sailor before he came land-seeking to western Canada.

After having "proved up" his land in southern Manitoba—the *Wanderlust* seized him and he went to South America, where no doubt he enlivened the proceedings for the natives, as he had for us while he lived among us.

Six weeks after the declaration of war he came back—a grizzled man of forty; he had sold out everything, sent his wife to England, and had come to enlist with the local regiment. Evidently his speech about what we owe to the Old Flag had been a piece of real eloquence, and Bill himself was the proof.

He enlisted with the boys from home as a private, and on the marches he towered above them—the tallest man in the regiment. No man was more obedient or trustworthy. He cheered and admonished the younger men, when long marches in the hot sun, with heavy accouterments, made them quarrelsome and full of complaints. "It's all for the Old Flag, boys," he told them.

To-day I read that he is "missing, believed killed"; and I have the feeling, which I know is in the heart of many who read his name, that we did not realize the heroism of the big fellow in the old days of peace. It took a war to show us how heroic our people are.

Not all the heroes are war-heroes either. The slow-grinding, searching tests of peace have found out some truly great ones among our people and have transmuted their common clay into pure gold.

It is much more heartening to tell of the woman who went right rather than of her who went wrong, and for that reason I gladly set down here the story of one of these.

Mrs. Elizabeth Tweed is the wife of Private William Tweed—small, dark-eyed, and pretty, with a certain childishness of face which makes her rouged cheeks and blackened eyebrows seem pathetically, innocently wicked.

Mrs. Elizabeth Tweed, wife of Private William Tweed, was giving trouble to the Patriotic Society. It was bad enough for her to go out evenings with an officer, and dance in the afternoon at the hotel *dansant* in a perfect outburst of gay garments; but there was no excuse for her coming home in a taxi-cab, after a shopping expedition in broad daylight, and to the scandal of the whole street, who watched her from behind lace curtains.

The evil effects of Mrs. Tweed's actions began to show in the falling-off of subscriptions to the Patriotic Fund, and the collectors heard many complaints about her gay habits of life and her many and varied ways of squandering money. Mrs. Tweed became a perfect wall of defense for those who were not too keen on parting with their money. They made a moral issue of it, and virtuously declared, "That woman is not going to the devil on my money." "I scrimp and save and deny myself everything so I can give to the Patriotic Fund, and look at her!" women cried.

It was in vain that the collectors urged that she was only getting five dollars a month, anyway, from the Patriotic Fund, and that would not carry her far on the road to destruction or in any other direction. When something which appears to set aside the obligation to perform a disagreeable duty comes in view, the hands of the soul naturally clamp on it.

Mrs. Tweed knew that she was the bad example, and gloried in it. She banged the front door when she entered the block late at night, and came up the stairs gayly singing, "Where did Robinson Crusoe go with Friday on Saturday night?" while her sleepy neighbors anathematized all dependents of the Patriotic Fund.

The Red Cross ladies discussed the matter among themselves and decided that some one should put the matter before Mrs. Tweed and tell her how hard she was making it for the other dependents of soldiers. The president was selected for the task, which did not at first sight look like a pleasant one, but Mrs. Kent had done harder things than this, and she set out bravely to call on the wayward lady.

The D.O.E. visitor who called on all the soldiers' wives in that block had reported that Mrs. Tweed had actually put her out, and told her to go to a region which is never mentioned in polite society except in theological discussions.

"I know," Mrs. Tweed said, when the Red Cross President came to see her, "what you are coming for, and I don't blame you—I sure have been fierce, but you don't know what a good time I've had. Gee, it's great! I've had one grand tear!—one blow-out! And now I am almost ready to be good. Sit down, and I'll tell you about it; you have more give to you than that old hatchet-face that came first; I wouldn't tell her a thing!

"I am twenty-five years old, and I never before got a chance to do as I liked. When I was a kid, I had to do as I was told. My mother brought me up in the fear of the Lord and the fear of the neighbors. I whistled once in church and was sent to bed every afternoon for a week—I didn't care, though, I got in my whistle. I never wanted to do anything bad, but I wanted to do as I liked—and I never got a chance. Then I got married. William is a lot older than I am, and he controlled me—always—made me economize, scrimp, and save. I really did not want to blow money, but they never gave me a chance to be sensible. Every one put me down for a 'nut.' My mother called me 'Trixie.' No girl can do well on a name like that. Teachers passed me from hand to hand saying, 'Trixie is such a mischief!' I had a reputation to sustain.

"Then mother and father married me off to Mr. Tweed because he was so sensible, and I needed a firm hand, they said. I began everything in life with a handicap. Name and appearance have always been against me. No one can look sensible with a nose that turns straight up, and I will have bright colors to wear—I was brought up on wincey, color of mud, and all these London-smoke, battleship-gray colors make me sick. I want reds and blues and greens, and I am gradually working into them."

She held out a dainty foot as she spoke, exhibiting a bright-green stocking striped in gold.

"But mind you, for all I am so frivolous, I am not a fool exactly. All I ask is to have my fling, and I've had it now for three whole months. When William was at home I never could sit up and read one minute, and so the first night he was away I burned the light all night just to feel wicked! It was great to be able to let it burn. I've gone to bed early every night for a week to make up for it. What do you think of that? It is just born in me, and I can't help it. If William had stayed at home, this would never have showed out in me. I would have gone on respectable and steady. But this is one of the prices we pay for bringing up women to be men's chattels, with some one always placed in authority over them. When the authority is removed, there's the devil to pay!"

The President of the Red Cross looked at her in surprise. She had never thought of it this way before; women were made to be protected and shielded; she had said so scores of times; the church had taught it and sanctioned it.

"The whole system is wrong," Mrs. Tweed continued, "and nice women like you, working away in churches ruled by men, have been to blame. You say women should be protected, and you cannot make good the protection. What protection have the soldiers' wives now? Evil tongues, prying eyes, on the part of women, and worse than that from the men. The church has fallen down on its job, and isn't straight enough to admit it! We should either train our women to take their own part and run their own affairs, or else we should train the men really to honor and protect women. The church has done neither. Bah! I could make a better world with one hand tied behind my back!"

"But, Mrs. Tweed," said the president, "this war is new to all of us— how did we know what was coming? It has taken all of us by surprise, and we have to do our bit in meeting the new conditions. Your man was never a fighting man—he hates it; but he has gone and will fight, although he loathes it. I never did a day's work outside of my home until now, and now I go to the office every day and try to straighten out tangles; women come in there and accuse me of everything, down to taking the bread out of their children's mouths. Two of them who brought in socks the other day said, 'Do you suppose the soldiers ever see them?' I did all I could to convince them that we were quite honest, though I assure you I felt like telling them what I thought of them. But things are abnormal now, everything is out of sorts; and if we love our country we will try to remedy things instead of making them worse. When I went to school we were governed by what they called the 'honor system.' It was a system of self-government; we were not watched and punished and bound by rules, but graded and ruled ourselves—and the strange thing about it was that it worked! When the teacher went out of the room, everything went on just the same. Nobody left her desk or talked or idled; we just worked on, minding our own affairs; it was a great system."

Mrs. Tweed looked at her with a cynical smile. "Some system!" she cried mockingly; "it may work in a school, where the little pinafore, pig-tail Minnies and Lucys gather; it won't work in life, where every one is grabbing for what he wants, and getting it some way. But see here," she cried suddenly, "you haven't called me down yet! or told me I am a disgrace to the Patriotic Fund! or asked me what will my husband say when he comes home! You haven't looked shocked at one thing I've told you. Say, you should have seen old hatchet-face when I told her that I hoped the war would last forever! She said I was a wicked woman!"

"Well—weren't you?" asked the president.

"Sure I was—if I meant it—but I didn't. I wanted to see her jump, and she certainly jumped; and she soon gave me up and went back and reported. Then you were sent, and I guess you are about ready to give in."

"Indeed, I am not," said the president, smiling. "You are not a fool—I can see that—and you can think out these things for yourself. You are not accountable to me, anyway. I have no authority to find fault with you. If you think your part in this terrible time is to go the limit in fancy clothes, theaters, and late suppers with men of questionable character—that is for you to decide. I believe in the honor system. You are certainly setting a bad example—but you have that privilege. You cannot be sent to jail for it. The money you draw is hard-earned money—it is certainly sweated labor which our gallant men perform for the miserable little sum that is paid them. It is yours to do with as you like. I had hoped that more of you young women would have come to help us in our work in the Red Cross and other places. We need your youth, your enthusiasm, your prettiness, for we are sorely pressed with many cares and troubles, and we seem to be old sometimes. But you are quite right in saying that it is your own business how you spend the money!"

After Mrs. Kent had gone, the younger woman sat looking around her flat with a queer feeling of discontent. A half-eaten box of chocolates was on the table and a new silk sweater coat lay across the lounge. In the tiny kitchenette a tap dripped with weary insistence, and unwashed dishes filled the sink. She got up suddenly and began to wash the dishes, and did not stop until every corner of her apartment was clean and tidy.

"I am getting dippy," she said as she looked at herself in the mirror in the buffet; "I've got to get out—this quiet life gets me. I'll go down to the *dansant* this afternoon—no use—I can't stand being alone."

She put on her white suit, and dabbing rouge on her cheeks and penciling her eyes, she went forth into the sunshiny streets.

She stopped to look at a display of sport suits in a window, also to see her own reflection in a mirror placed for the purpose among the suits.

Suddenly a voice sounded at her elbow: "Some kid, eh? Looking good enough to eat!"

She turned around and met the admiring gaze of Sergeant Edward Loftus Brown, recruiting sergeant of the 19-th, with whom she had been to the theater a few nights before. She welcomed him effusively.

"Come on and have something to eat," he said. "I got three recruits to-day—so I am going to proclaim a half-holiday."

They sat at a table in an alcove and gayly discussed the people who passed by. The President of the Red Cross came in, and at a table across the room hastily drank a cup of tea and went out again.

"She came to see me to-day," said Mrs. Tweed, "and gave me to understand that they were not any too well pleased with me—I am too gay for a soldier's wife! And they do not approve of you."

34

Sergeant Brown smiled indulgently and looked at her admiringly through his oyster-lidded eyes. His smile was as complacent as that of the ward boss who knows that the ballot-box is stuffed. It was the smile of one who can afford to be generous to an enemy.

"Women are always hard on each other," he said soothingly; "these women do not understand you, Trixie, that's all. No person understands you but me." His voice was of the magnolia oil quality.

"Oh, rats!" she broke out. "Cut that understanding business! She understands me all right—she knows me for a mean little selfish slacker who is going to have a good time no matter what it costs. I have been like a bad kid that eats the jam when the house is burning! But remember this, I'm no fool, and I'm not going to kid myself into thinking it is anything to be proud of, for it isn't."

Sergeant Brown sat up straight and regarded her critically. "What have you done," he said, "that she should call you down for it? You're young and pretty and these old hens are jealous of you. They can't raise a good time themselves and they're sore on you because all the men are crazy about you."

"Gee, you're mean," Mrs. Tweed retorted, "to talk that way about women who are giving up everything for their country. Mrs. Kent's two boys are in the trenches, actually fighting, not just parading round in uniform like you. She goes every day and works in the office of the Red Cross and tries to keep every tangle straightened out. She's not jealous of me—she despises me for a little feather-brained pinhead. She thinks I am even worse than I am. She thinks I am as bad as you would like me to be! Naturally enough, she judges me by my company."

Sergeant Brown's face flushed dull red, but she went on: "That woman is all right—take it from me."

"Well, don't get sore on me," he said quickly; "I'm not the one who is turning you down. I've always stuck up for you and you know it!"

"Why shouldn't you?" she cried. "You know well that I am straight, even if I am a fool. These women are out of patience with me and my class——"

"Men are always more charitable to women than women are to each other, anyway—women are cats, mostly!" he said, as he rolled a cigarette.

"There you go again!" she cried,—"pretending that you know. I tell you women are women's best friends. What help have you given to me to run straight, for all your hot air about thinking so much of me? You've stuck around my flat until I had to put you out—you've never sheltered or protected me in any way. Men are broad-minded toward women's

35

characters because they do not care whether women are good or not—they would rather that they were not. I do not mean all men,—William was different, and there are plenty like him—but I mean men like you who run around with soldiers' wives and slam the women who are our friends, and who are really concerned about us. You are twenty years older than I am. You're always blowing about how much you know about women—also the world. Why didn't you advise me not to make a fool of myself?"

Sergeant Brown leaned over and patted her hand. "There now, Trixie," he said, "don't get excited; you're the best girl in town, only you're too high-strung. Haven't I always stood by you? Did I ever turn you down, even when these high-brow ladies gave you the glassy eye? Why are you going back on a friend now? You had lots to say about the Daughter of the Empire who came to see you the last time."

"She wasn't nice to me," said Mrs. Tweed; "but she meant well, anyway. But I'm getting ashamed of myself now—for I see I am not playing the game. Things have gone wrong through no fault of ours. The whole world has gone wrong, and it's up to us to bring it right if we can. These women are doing their share—they've given up everything. But what have I done? I let William go, of course, and that's a lot, for I do think a lot of William; but I am not doing my own share. Running around to the stores, eating late suppers, saying snippy things about other women, and giving people an excuse for not giving to the Patriotic Fund. You and I sitting here to-day, eating expensive things, are not helping to win the war, I can tell you."

"But my dear girl," he interrupted, "whose business is it? and what has happened to you anyway? I didn't bring you here to tell me my patriotic duty. I like you because you amuse me with your smart speeches. I don't want to be lectured—and I won't have it."

Mrs. Tweed arose and began to put on her gloves. "Here's where we part," she said; "I am going to begin to do my part, just as I see it. I've signed on—I've joined the great Win-the-War-Party. You should try it, Sergeant Brown. We have no exact rules to go by—we are self-governed. It is called the honor system; each one rules himself. It's quite new to me, but I expect to know more about it."

"Sit down!" he said sternly; "people are looking at you—they think we are quarreling; I am not done yet, and neither are you. Sit down!"

She sat down and apologized. "I am excited, I believe," she said; "people generally are when they enlist; and although I stood up, I had no intention of going, for the bill has not come yet and I won't go without settling my share of it."

"Forget it!" he said warmly; "this isn't a Dutch treat. What have I done that you should hit me a slam like this?"

"It isn't a slam," she said; "it is quite different. I want to run straight and fair—and I can't do it and let you pay for my meals; there's no sense in women being sponges. I know we have been brought up to beat our way. 'Be pretty, and all things will be added unto you,' is the first commandment, and the one with the promise. I've laid hold on that all my life, but to-day I am giving it up. The old way of training women nearly got me, but not quite—and now I am making a new start. It isn't too late. The old way of women always being under an obligation to men has started us wrong. I'm not blaming you or any one, but I'm done with it. If you see things as I do, you'll be willing to let me pay. Don't pauperize me any more and make me feel mean."

"Oh, go as far as you like!" he said petulantly. "Pay for me, too, if you like—don't leave me a shred of self-respect. This all comes of giving women the vote. I saw it coming, but I couldn't help it! I like the old-fashioned women best—but don't mind me!"

"I won't," she said; "nothing is the same as it was. How can anything go on the same? We have to change to meet new conditions and I'm starting to-day. I'm going to give up my suite and get a job—anything—maybe dishwashing. I'm going to do what I can to bring things right. If every one will do that, the country is safe."

In a certain restaurant there is a little waitress with clustering black hair and saucy little turned-up nose. She moves quickly, deftly, decidedly, and always knows what to do. She is young, pretty, and bright, and many a man has made up his mind to speak to her and ask her to "go out and see a show"; but after exchanging a few remarks with her, he changes his mind. Something tells him it would not go! She carries trays of dishes from eight-thirty to six every day except Sunday. She has respectfully refused to take her allowance from the Patriotic Fund, explaining that she has a job. The separation allowance sent to her from the Militia Department at Ottawa goes directly into the bank, and she is able to add to it sometimes from her wages.

The people in the block where Mrs. Tweed lived will tell you that she suddenly gave up her suite and moved away and they do not know where she went, but they are very much afraid she was going "wrong." What a lot of pleasant surprises there will be for people when they get to heaven!

CHAPTER VII
CONSERVATION

There are certain words which have come into general circulation since the war. One of the very best of these is "Conservation."

Conservation is a fine, rich-sounding, round word, agreeable to the ear and eye, and much more aristocratic than the word "Reform," which seems to carry with it the unpleasant suggestion of something that needs to be changed. The dictionary, which knows everything, says that "Conservation means the saving from destructive change the good we already possess," which seems to be a perfectly worthy ambition for any one to entertain.

For many people, changes have in them an element of wickedness and danger. I once knew a little girl who wore a sunbonnet all summer and a hood all winter, and cried one whole day each spring and fall when she had to make the change; for changes to her were fearsome things.

This antagonism to change has delayed the progress of the world and kept back many a needed reform, for people have grown to think that whatever is must be right, and indeed have made a virtue of this belief.

"It was good enough for my father and it is good enough for me," cries many a good tory (small *t*, please), thinking that by this utterance he convinces an admiring world that all his folks have been exceedingly fine people for generations.

But changes are inevitable. What is true to-day may not be true to-morrow. All our opinions should be marked, "Subject to change without notice." We cannot all indulge ourselves in the complacency of the maiden lady who gave her age year after year as twenty-seven, because she said she was not one of these flighty things who say "one thing to-day and something else to-morrow."

Life is change. Only dead things remain as they are. Every living thing feels the winds of the world blowing over it, beating and buffeting it, marking and bleaching it. Change is a characteristic of life, and we must reckon on it! Progress is Life's first law! In order to be as good as we were yesterday, we have to be better. Life is built on a sliding scale; we have to keep moving to keep up. There are no rest stations on Life's long road!

The principle of conservation is not at enmity with the spirit of change. It is in thorough harmony with it.

Conservation becomes a timely topic in these days of hideous waste. In fact it will not much longer remain among the optional subjects in Life's curriculum. Even now the Moving Finger, invisible yet to the thoughtless, is writing after it the stern word "Compulsory." Four hundred thousand men have been taken away from the ranks of producers here in Canada, and have gone into the ranks of destroyers, becoming a drain upon our resources for all that they eat, wear, and use. Many thousand other men are making munitions, whose end is destruction and waste. We spend more in a day now to kill and hurt our fellow men than we ever spent in a month to educate or help them. Great new ways of wasting and destroying our resources are going on while the old leaks are all running wide open. More children under five years old have died since the war than there have been men killed in battle!—and largely from preventable "dirt-diseases" and poverty. Rats, weeds, extravagance, general shiftlessness are still doing business at the old stand, unmolested.

But it is working in on us that something must be done. Now is the time to set in force certain agencies to make good these losses in so far as they can be repaired. Now is the time, when the excitement of the war is still on us, when the frenzy is still in our blood, for the time of reaction is surely to be reckoned with by and by. Now we are sustained by the blare of the bands and the flourish of flags, but in the cold, gray dawn of the morning after, we shall count our dead with disillusioned eyes and wonder what was the use of all this bloodshed and waste. Trade conditions are largely a matter of the condition of the spirit, and ours will be drooping and drab when the tumult and the shouting have died and the reign of reason has come back.

Personal thrift comes naturally to our minds when we begin to think of the lessons that we should take to heart. Up to the time of the war and since, we have been a prodigal people, confusing extravagance with generosity, thrift with meanness. The Indians in the old days killed off the buffalo for the sport of killing, and left the carcases to rot, never thinking of a time of want; and so, too, the natives in the North Country kill the caribou for the sake of their tongues, which are considered a real "company dish," letting the remainder of the animal go to waste.

This is a startling thought, and comes to one over and over again. You will think of it when you order your twenty-five cents' worth of cooked

39

ham and see what you get! You will think of it again when you come home and find that the butcher delivered your twenty-five cents' worth of cooked ham in your absence, and, finding the door locked, passed it through the keyhole. And yet the prodigality of the Indian and the caribou-killer are infantile compared with the big extravagances that go on without much comment. Economy is a broad term used to express the many ways in which other people might save money. Members of Parliament have been known to tell many ways in which women might economize; their tender hearts are cut to the quick as they notice the fancy footwear and expensive millinery worn by women. Great economy meetings have been held in London, to which the Cabinet Ministers rode in expensive cars, and where they drank champagne, enjoining women to abjure the use of veils and part with their pet dogs as a war measure; but they said not a word about the continuance of the liquor business which rears its head in every street and has wasted three million tons of grain since the war began. What wonder is it that these childish appeals to the women to economize fall on deaf or indignant ears! Women have a nasty way of making comparisons. They were so much easier to manage before they learned to read and write.

The war wears on its weary course. The high cost of living becomes more and more of a nightmare to the people, yet the British Government tolerates a system which wastes more sugar than would feed the army, impairs the efficiency of the working-man one sixth, and wastes two million dollars every day in what is at best a questionable indulgence, and at worst a national menace. Speaking of economy, personal thrift, conservation, and other "win-the-war" plans, how would the elimination of the liquor traffic do for a start?

There are two ways of practicing economy: one is by refusing to spend money, which is not always a virtue; and the other is by increasing production, which is the greatest need of this critical time. The farmers are doing all they can: they are producing as much as they have means and labor for. But still in Canada much land is idle, and many people sit around wondering what they can do. There will be women sitting on verandas in the cities and towns in the summer, knitting socks, or maybe crocheting edges on handkerchiefs, who would gladly be raising potatoes and chickens if they knew how to begin; and a corresponding number of chickens and potatoes will go unraised. But the idea of coöperation is taking root, and here and there there is a breaking away from the conventional mode of life. The best thing about it is that people are thinking, and pretty soon the impact of public opinion will be so strong that there will be a national movement to bring together the idle people and the idle land. We are paying a high price for our tuition, but we must admit that the war is a great teacher.

There is a growing sentiment against the holding-up of tracts of land by speculators waiting for the increase in value which comes by the hard work of settlers. Every sod turned by the real, honest settler, who comes to make his home, increases the value of the section of land next him, probably held by a railway company, and the increase makes it harder for some other settler to buy it. By his industry the settler makes money for the railway company, but incidentally makes his own chance of acquiring a neighbor more remote!

The wild-lands tax which prevails in the western provinces of the Dominion, and which we hope will be increased, will make it unprofitable to hold land idle, and will do much, if made heavy enough, to liberate land for settlement.

As it is now, people who have no money to buy land have to go long distances from the railroad to get homesteads, and there suffer all the inconveniences and hardships and dangers of pioneer life, miles from neighbors, many miles from a doctor, and without school or church; while great tracts of splendid land lie idle and unimproved, close beside the little towns, held in the tight clasp of a hypothetical owner far away.

Western Canada has a land problem which war conditions have intensified. But people are beginning to talk of these things, and the next few years will see radical changes.

The coming of women into the political world should help. Women are born conservationists. Their first game is housekeeping and doll-mending. The doll, by preference, is a sick doll, and in need of care. Their work is to care for, work for something, and if the advent of women into politics does not mean that life is made easier and safer for other women and for children, then we will have to confess with shame and sorrow that politically we have failed! But we are not going to fail! Already the angel has come down and has troubled the water. Discussions are raging in women's societies and wherever women meet together, and out of it something will come. Men are always quite willing to be guided by women when their schemes are sound and sane.

In New Zealand the first political activity of women was directed toward lowering the death-rate among children, by sending out trained nurses to care for them and give instruction to the mothers. Ours will follow the same line, because the heart of woman is the same everywhere. Dreams will soon begin to come true. Good dreams always do—in time; and why not? There is nothing too good to be true! Here is one that is coming!

41

Little Mary Wood set out bravely to do the chores; for it was Christmas Eve, and even in the remoteness of the Abilene Valley, some of the old-time festivity of Christmas was felt. Mary's mother had had good times at Christmas when she was a little girl, and Mary's imagination did the rest. Mary started out singing.

It was a mean wind that came through the valley that night; a wind that took no notice of Christmas, or Sunday, or even of the brave little girl doing the chores, so that her father might not have them to do when he came home. It was so mean that it would not even go round Mary Wood, aged eleven, and small for her age—it went straight through her and chattered her teeth and blued her hands, and would have frozen her nose if she had not at intervals put her little hand over it.

But in spite of the wind, the chores were done at last, and Mary came back to the house. Mary's mother was always waiting to open the door and shut it quick again, but to-night, when Mary reached the door she had to open it herself, for her mother had gone to bed.

Mary was surprised at this, and hastened to the bedroom to see what was wrong.

Mary's mother replied to her questions quite cheerfully. She was not sick. She was only tired. She would be all right in the morning. But Mary Wood, aged eleven, had grown wise in her short years, and she knew there was something wrong. Never mind; she would ask father. He always knew everything and what to do about it.

Going back to the kitchen she saw the writing-pad on which her mother had been writing. Her mother did not often write letters; certainly did not often tear them up after writing them; and here in the home-made waste-paper basket was a torn and crumpled sheet. Mary did not know that it was not the square thing to read other people's letters, and, besides, she wanted to know. She spread the letter on the table and pieced it together. Laboriously she spelled it out:—

"I don't know why I am so frightened this time, Lizzie, but I am black afraid. I suppose it is because I lost the other two. I hate this lonely, God-forsaken country. I am afraid of it to-night—it's so big and white and far away, and it seems as if nobody cares. Mary does not know, and I cannot tell her; but I know I should, for she may be left with the care of Bobbie. To-night I am glad the other two are safe. It is just awful to be a woman, Lizzie; women get it going and coming, and the worst of it is, no one cares!"

Mary read the letter over and over, before she grasped its meaning. Then the terrible truth rolled over her, and her heart seemed to stop beating. Mary had not lived her eleven years without finding out some of

42

the grim facts of life. She knew that the angels brought babies at very awkward times, and to places where they were not wanted a bit, and she also knew that sometimes, when they brought a baby, they had been known to take the mother away. Mary had her own opinion of the angels who did that, but it had been done. There was only one hope: her father always knew what to do.

She thawed a hole in the frosted window and tried to see down the trail, but the moon was foggy and it was impossible to see more than a few yards.

Filled with a sense of fear and dread, she built up a good fire and filled the kettle with water; she vigorously swept the floor and tidied the few books on their home-made shelf.

It was ten o'clock when her father came in, pale and worried. Mary saw that he knew, too.

He went past her into the bedroom and spoke hurriedly to his wife; but Mary did not hear what they said.

Suddenly she heard her mother cry and instinctively she ran into the room.

Her father stood beside the bed holding his head, as if in pain. Mary's mother had turned her face into the pillow, and cried; and even little Bobbie, who had been awakened by the unusual commotion, sat up, rubbing his eyes, and cried softly to himself.

Mary's father explained it to Mary.

"Mrs. Roberts has gone away," he said. "I went over to see her to-day. We were depending on her to come over and take care of your mother—for a while—and now she has gone, and there is not another woman between here and the Landing."

"It's no use trying, Robert," Mrs. Wood said between her sobs; "I can't stay—I am so frightened. I am beginning to see things—and I know what it means. There are black things in every corner—trying to tell me something, grinning, jabbering things—that are waiting for me; I see them everywhere I look."

Mr. Wood sat down beside her, and patted her hand.

"I know, dear," he said; "it's hell, this lonely life. It's too much for any woman, and I'll give it all up. Better to live on two meals a day in a city than face things like this. We wanted a home of our own, Millie,—you remember how we used to talk,—and we thought we had found it here—good land and a running stream. We have worked hard and it is just beginning to pay, but we'll have to quit—and I'll have to work for some one else all my life. It was too good to be true, Millie."

He spoke without any bitterness in his voice, just a settled sadness, and a great disappointment.

Suddenly the old dog began to bark with strong conviction in every bark, which indicated that he had really found something at last that was worth mentioning. There was a sudden jangle of sleighbells in the yard, and Mary's father went hastily to the door and called to the dog to be quiet. A woman walked into the square of light thrown on the snow from the open door, and asked if this was the place where a nurse was needed.

Mr. Wood reached out and took her big valise and brought her into the house, too astonished to speak. He was afraid she might vanish.

She threw off her heavy coat before she spoke, and then, as she wiped the frost from her eyebrows, she explained:—

"I am what is called a pioneer nurse, and I am sent to take care of your wife, as long as she needs me. You see the women in Alberta have the vote now, and they have a little more to say about things than they used to have, and one of the things they are keen on is to help pioneer women over their rough places. Your neighbor, Mrs. Roberts, on her way East, reported your wife's case, and so I am here. The Mounted Police brought me out, and I have everything that is needed."

"But I don't understand!" Mr. Wood began.

"No!" said the nurse; "it is a little queer, isn't it? People have spent money on pigs and cattle and horses, and have bonused railways and elevator companies, or anything that seemed to help the country, while the people who were doing the most for the country, the settlers' wives, were left to live or die as seemed best to them. Woman's most sacred function is to bring children into the world, and if all goes well, why, God bless her!—but when things go wrong—God help her! No one else was concerned at all. But, as I told you, women vote now in Alberta, and what they say goes. Men are always ready to help women in any good cause, but, naturally enough, they don't see the tragedy of the lonely woman, as women see it. They are just as sympathetic, but they do not know what to do. Some time ago, before the war, there was an agitation to build a monument to the pioneer women, a great affair of marble and stone. The women did not warm up to it at all. They pointed out that it was poor policy to build monuments to brave women who had died, while other equally brave women in similar circumstances were being let die! So they sort of frowned down the marble monument idea, and began to talk of nurses instead.

"So here I am," concluded Mrs. Sanderson, as she hung up her coat and cap. "I am a monument to those who are gone, and the free gift of the people of Alberta to you and your wife, in slight appreciation of the work

44

you are doing in settling the country and making all the land in this district more valuable. They are a little late in acknowledging what they owe the settler, but it took the women a few years to get the vote, and then a little while longer to get the woman's point of view before the public."

Mary Wood stood at her father's side while the nurse spoke, drinking in every word.

"But who pays?" asked Mary's father—"who pays for this?"

"It is all simple enough," said the nurse. "There are many millions of acres in Alberta held by companies, and by private owners, who live in New York, London, and other places, who hold this land idle, waiting for the prices to go up. The prices advance with the coming-in of settlers like yourself, and these owners get the benefit. The Government thinks these landowners should be made to pay something toward helping the settlers, so they have put on a wild-lands tax of one per cent of the value of the land; they have also put a telephone tax on each unoccupied section, which will make it as easy for you to get a telephone as if every section was settled; and they have also a hospital tax, and will put up a hospital next year, where free treatment will be given to every one who belongs to the municipality.

"The idea is to tax the wild land so heavily that it will not be profitable for speculators to hold it, and it will be released for real, sure-enough settlers. The Government holds to the view that it is better to make homes for many people than to make fortunes for a few people."

Mary's father sat down with a great sigh that seemed half a laugh and half a sob.

"What is it you said the women have now?" asked Mary.

The nurse explained carefully to her small but interested audience. When she was done, Mary Wood, aged eleven, had chosen her life-work.

"Now I know what I'll be when I grow big," she said; "I intended to be a missionary, but I've changed my mind—I am going to be a Voter!"

CHAPTER VIII

"PERMISSION"

He walked among us many years, And yet we failed to understand
That there was courage in his fears And strength within his gentle hand:
We did not mean to be unkind, But we were dull of heart and mind!

. . . .

But when the drum-beat through the night And men were called, with
voice austere, To die for England's sake—and right, He was the first to
answer, "Here!" His courage, long submerged, arose, When at her gates,
knocked England's foes!

. . . .

And so to-day, where the brave dead Sleep sweetly amid Flemish
bowers, One grave, in thought, is garlanded With prairie flowers!

And if the dead in realms of bliss Can think on those they knew below,
He'll know we're sorry, and that this Is our poor way of saying so!

The war has put a new face on our neighborhood life; it has searched
out and tried the hidden places of our souls, and strange, indeed, have
been its findings. By its severe testings some of those who we thought
were our strongest people have been abased, and some of the weak ones
have been exalted. There were some of our people who were good
citizens in the normal times of peace, but who could not stand against the
sterner test of war; and then again we have found the true worth of some
of those whom in our dull, short-sighted way we did not know!

Stanley Goodman came to our neighborhood when he was a lad of
sixteen. The Church of England clergyman, who knew his people in
England, brought him to Mrs. Corbett, who kept the Black Creek
Stopping House, and asked her if she could give him a room and look
after him. He told her of the great wealth and social position of the
family who were willing to pay well for the boy's keep.

"If they are as well off as all that," said Mrs. Corbett, "why are they
sending the wee lad out here, away from all of them?"

The clergyman found it hard to explain. "It seems that this boy is not
quite like the other members of the family—not so bright, I take it," he
said; "and the father particularly is a bit disappointed in him!"

"Do you mean," said Mrs. Corbett, "that they are ashamed of the poor
little fellow, and are sending him out here to get rid of him? Faith, if
that's the kind of heathen there is in England I don't know why they send
missionaries out here to preach to us. Bad and all as we are, there is none
of us that would do the like of that!"

46

"They will provide handsomely for him in every way, Mrs. Corbett, and leave no wish ungratified," the minister said uneasily.

Mrs. Corbett was a difficult person in some ways.

"Oh, sure, they will give him everything but love and home, and that'll be what the poor wee lad will hunger for! Money is a queer thing for sure, when it will make a mother forget the child that she brought into the world!"

"I think the mother—from what I can gather—wanted to keep the boy, but the father is a very proud man, and this lad aggravated him some way just to see him, and the mother yielded to his wishes, as a true wife should, and for the sake of peace has withdrawn her objections."

"A poor soft fool, that's all she is, to let a domineering old reprobate send her poor lad away, just because he did not like to see him around, and him his own child! And even you, Mr. Tilton, who have been out here living with civilized people for three years, have enough of the old country way in you yet to say that a true wife should consent to this to please the old tyrant! Faith, I don't blame the Suffragettes for smashing windows, and if I wasn't so busy feeding hungry men, I believe I would go over and give them a hand, only I would be more careful what I was smashing and would not waste my time on innocent windows!"

"But you will take him, won't you, Mrs. Corbett? I will feel quite easy about him if you will!"

"I suppose I'll have to. I can't refuse when his own have deserted him! I would be a poor member of the Army if I did not remember Our Lord's promise to the poor children when their fathers and mothers forsake them, and I will try to carry it out as well as I can."

Stanley was soon established in the big white-washed room in Mrs. Corbett's boarding-house. He brought with him everything that any boy could ever want, and his room, which he kept spotlessly clean, with its beautiful rug, pictures, and books, was the admiration of the neighborhood.

Stanley understood the situation and spoke of it quite frankly.

"My father thought it better for me to come away for a while, to see if it would not toughen me up a bit. He has been rather disappointed in me, I think. You see, I had an accident when I was a little fellow and since then I have not been—quite right."

"Just think of that," Mrs. Corbett said afterwards in telling it to a sympathetic group of "Stoppers." "It wouldn't be half so bad if the poor boy didn't know that he is queer. I tried to reason it out of him, but he said that he had heard the housekeeper and the parlor-maid at home talking of it, and they said he was a bit looney. It wouldn't be half so bad for him if he was not so near to being all right! If ever I go wrong in the head I hope I'll be so crazy that I won't know that I'm crazy. Craziness is like everything else—it's all right if you have enough of it!"

"Stanley is not what any one would call crazy," said one of the Stoppers; "the only thing I can see wrong with him is that you always know what he is going to say, and he is too polite, and every one can fool him! He certainly is a good worker, and there's another place he shows that he is queer, for he doesn't need to work and still he does it! He likes it, and thanked me to-day for letting him clean my team; and as a special favor I'm going to let him hitch them up when I am ready to go!"

Stanley busied himself about the house, and was never so happy as when he was rendering some service to some one. But even in his happiest moments there was always the wistful longing for home, and when he was alone with Mrs. Corbett he freely spoke of his hopes and fears.

"It may not be so long before they begin to think that they would like to see me; do you think that it is really true that absence makes the heart grow fonder—even of people—like me? I keep thinking that maybe they will send for me after a while and let me stay for a few days anyway. My mother will want to see me, I am almost sure,—indeed, she almost said as much,—and she said many times that she hoped that I would be quite happy; and when I left she kissed me twice, and even the governor shook hands with me and said, 'You will be all right out there in Canada.' He was so nice with me, it made it jolly hard to leave."

Another day, as he dried the dishes for her, assuring her that it was a real joy for him to be let do this, he analyzed the situation again:—

"My father's people are all very large and handsome," he said, "and have a very commanding way with them; my father has always been obeyed, and always got what he wanted. It was my chin which bothered him the most. It is not much of a chin, I know; it retreats, doesn't it? But I cannot help it. But I have always been a bitter disappointment to him, and it really has been most uncomfortable for mother—he seemed to blame her some way, too; and often and often I found her looking at me so sadly and saying, 'Poor Stanley!' and all my aunts, when they came to visit, called me that. It was—not pleasant."

Every week his letter came from home, with books and magazines and everything that a boy could wish for. His delight knew no bounds. "They must think something of me," he said over and over again! At first he wrote a letter to his mother every day, but a curt note came from his father one day telling him that he must try to interest himself in his surroundings and that it would be better if he wrote only once a week!

The weekly letter then became an event, and he copied it over many times. Mrs. Corbett, busy with her work of feeding the traveling public, often paused long enough in her work of peeling the potatoes or rolling out pie-crust to wipe her hands hastily and read the letter that he had written and pass judgment on it.

Feeling that all green Englishmen were their legitimate prey for sport, the young bloods of the neighborhood, led by Pat Brennan, Mrs. Corbett's nephew, began to tell Stanley strange and terrible stories of Indians, and got him to send home for rifles and knives to defend himself and the neighborhood from their traitorous raids, "which were sure to be made on the settlements as soon as the cold weather came and the Indians got hungry." He was warned that he must not speak to Mrs. Corbett about this, for it is never wise to alarm the women. "We will have trouble enough without having a lot of hysterical women on our hands," said Pat.

After the weapons had come "The Exterminators" held a session behind closed doors to see what was the best plan of attack, and decided that they would not wait for the Indians to begin the trouble, but would make war on them. They decided that they would beat the bushes for Indians down in the river-bottom, while Stanley would sit at a certain point of vantage in a clump of willows, and as the Indians ran past him, he would pot them!

Stanley had consented to do this only after he had heard many tales of Indian treachery and cruelty to the settlers and their families!

The plan was carried out and would no doubt have been successful, but for the extreme scarcity of Indians in our valley.

All night long Stanley sat at his post, peering into the night, armed to the teeth, shivering with the cold wind that blew through the valley. His teeth chattered with fright sometimes, too, as the bushes rustled behind him, and an inquisitive old cow who came nosing the willows never knew how near death she had been. Meanwhile his traitorous companions went home and slept soundly and sweetly in their warm beds.

"And even after he found out that we were fooling him, he was not a bit sore," said Pat. "He tried to laugh! That is what made me feel cheap—he is too easy; it's too much like taking candy from a kid. And he was mighty square about it, too, and he never told Aunt Maggie how he got the cold, for he slipped into bed that morning and she didn't know he was out."

Another time the boys set him to gathering the puff-balls that grew in abundance in the hay meadow, assuring him that they were gopher-eggs and if placed under a hen would hatch out young gophers.

Stanley was wild with enthusiasm when he heard this and hastened to pack a box full to send home. "They *will* be surprised," he said. Fortunately, Mrs. Corbett found out about this before the box was sent, and she had to tell him that the boys were only in fun.

When she told him that the boys had been just having sport there came over his face such a look of sadness and pain, such a deeply hurt look, that Mrs. Corbett went back to the barn and thrashed her sturdy young nephew, all over again.

When the matter came up for discussion again, Stanley implored her not to speak of it any more, and not to hold it against the boys. "It was not their fault at all," he said; "it all comes about on account of my being—not quite right. I am not quite like other boys, but when they play with me I forget it and I believe what they say. There is—something wrong with me,—and it makes people want—to have sport with me; but it is not their fault at all."

"Well, they won't have sport with you when I am round," declared Mrs. Corbett stoutly.

Years rolled by and Stanley still cherished the hope that some day "permission" would come for him to go home. He grew very fast and became rather a fine-looking young man. Once, emboldened by a particularly kind letter from his mother, he made the request that he should be allowed to go home for a few days. "If you will let me come home even for one day, dearest mother," he wrote, "I will come right back content, and father will not need to see me at all. I want to stand once more before that beautiful Tissot picture of Christ holding the wounded lamb in his arms, and I would like to see the hawthorn hedge when it is in bloom as it will be soon, and above all, dear mother, I want to see you. And I will come directly away."

He held this letter for many days, and was only emboldened to send it by Mrs. Corbett's heartiest assurances that it was a splendid letter and that his mother would like it!

"I do not want to give my mother trouble," he said. "She has already had much trouble with me; but it might make her more content to see me and to know that I am so well—and happy."

After the letter had been sent, Stanley counted the days anxiously, and on the big map of Canada that hung on the kitchen wall he followed its course until it reached Halifax, and then his mind went with it tossing on the ocean.

"I may get my answer any day after Friday," he said. "Of course I do not expect it right off—it will take some little time for mother to speak to father, and, besides, he might not be at home; so I must not be disappointed if it seems long to wait."

Friday passed and many weeks rolled by, and still Stanley was hopeful. "They are considering," he said, "and that is so much better than if they refused; and perhaps they are looking about a boat—I think that must be what is keeping the letter back. I feel so glad and happy about it, it seems that permission must be coming."

In a month a bulky parcel came to him by express. It contained a framed picture of the Good Shepherd carrying the lost lamb in his arms; a box of hawthorn blossoms, faded but still fragrant, and a book which gave directions for playing solitaire in one hundred and twenty-three ways!!

Mrs. Corbett hastened to his room when she heard the cry of pain that escaped his lips. He stood in the middle of the floor with the book in his hand. All the boyishness had gone out of his face, which now had the spent look of one who has had a great fright or suffered great pain. The book on solitaire had pierced through his cloudy brain with the thought that his was a solitary part in life, and for a few moments he went through the panicky grief of the faithful dog who finds himself left on the shore while his false master sails gayly away!

"I will be all right directly," he stammered, making a pitiful effort to control his tears.

Mrs. Corbett politely appeared not to notice, and went hastily downstairs, and although not accustomed to the use of the pen, yet she took it in hand and wrote a letter to Stanley's father.

"It is a pity that your poor lad did not inherit some of your hardness of heart, Mr. Goodman," the letter began, "for if he did he would not be upstairs now breakin his and sobbin it out of him at your cruel answer to his natural request that he might go home and see his mother. But he has a heart of gold wherever he got it I don't know, and it is just a curse to him to be so constant in his love for home, when there is no love or welcome there for him. He is a lad that any man might well be proud of him, that gentle and kind and honest and truthful, not like most of the young doods that come out here drinkin and carousin and raisin the divil. mebbe you would like him better if he was and this is just to tell you that we like your boy here and we dont think much of the way you are using him and I hope that you will live to see the day that you will regret with tears more bitter than he is sheddin now the way you have treated him, and with these few lines I will close M corbett."

51

How this letter was received at Mayflower Lodge, Bucks, England, is not known, for no answer was ever sent; and although the letters to Stanley came regularly, his wish to go home was not mentioned in any of them. Neither did he ever refer to it again.

"Say, Stan," said young Pat one day, suddenly smitten with a bright thought, "why don't you go home anyway? You have lots of money—why don't you walk in on 'em and give 'em a surprise?"

"It would not be playing the game, Pat; thank you all the same, old chap," said Stanley heartily, "but I will not go home without permission."

After that Stanley got more and more reticent about the people at home. He seemed to realize that they had cut him off, but the homesick look never left his eyes. His friends now were the children of the neighborhood and the animals. Dogs, cats, horses, and children followed him, and gave him freely of their affection. He worked happy hours in Mrs. Corbett's garden, and "Stanley's flowers" were the admiration of the neighborhood.

When he was not busy in the garden, he spent long hours beside the river in a beautifully fashioned seat which he had made for himself, beneath a large poplar tree. "It is the wind in the tree-tops that I like," he said. "It whispers to me. I can't tell what it says, but it says something. I like trees—they are like people some way—only more patient and friendly."

The big elms and spruce of the river valley rustled and whispered together, and the poplars shook their coin-like leaves as he lay beneath their shade. The trees were trying to be kind to him, as the gray olive trees in Gethsemane were kind to One Other when his own had forgotten Him!

When the news of the war fell upon the Pembina Valley, it did not greatly disturb the peacefulness of that secluded spot. The well-to-do farmers who had held their grain over openly rejoiced at the prospect of better prices, and the younger men, when asked to enlist, replied by saying that the people who made the war had better do the fighting because they had no ambition to go out and stop German bullets. The general feeling was that it would soon be over.

At the first recruiting meeting Stanley volunteered his services by walking down the aisle of the church at the first invitation. The recruiting officer motioned to him to be seated, and that he would see him after the meeting.

Stanley waited patiently until every person was gone, and then timidly said, "And now, sir, will you please tell me what I am to do?"

The recruiting officer, a dapper little fellow, very pompous and important, turned him down mercilessly. Stanley was dismayed. He wandered idly out of the church and was about to start off on his four-mile walk to the Stopping House when a sudden impulse seized him and he followed the recruiting agent to the house where he was staying.

He overtook him just as he was going into the house, and, seizing him by the arm, cried, "Don't you see, sir, that you must take me? I am strong and able—I tell you I am no coward—what have you against me, I want to know?"

The recruiting officer hesitated. Confound it all! It is a hard thing to tell a man that he is not exactly right in the head.

But he did not need to say it, for Stanley beat him to it. "I know what's wrong," he said; "you think I'm not very bright—I am not, either. But don't you see, war is an elemental sort of thing. I can do what I'm told—and I can fight. What does it matter if my head is not very clear on some things which are easy to you? And don't you see how much I want to go? Life has not been so sweet that I should want to hold on to it. The young men here do not want to go, for they are having such a good time. But there is nothing ahead of me that holds me back. Can't you see that, sir? Won't you pass me on, anyway, and let me have my chance? Give me a trial; it's time enough to turn me down when I fail at something. Won't you take me, sir?"

The recruiting officer sadly shook his head. Stanley watched him in an agony of suspense. Here was his way out—his way of escape from this body of death that had hung over him ever since he could remember. He drew nearer to the recruiting officer,—"For God's sake, sir, take me!" he cried.

Then the recruiting officer pulled himself together and grew firm and commanding. "I won't take you," he said, "and that's all there is about it. This is a job for grown-up men and men with all their wits about them. You would faint at the sight of blood and cry when you saw the first dead man."

In a few weeks another recruiting meeting was held, and again Stanley presented himself when the first invitation was given. The recruiting officer remembered him, and rather impatiently told him to sit down. Near the front of the hall sat the German-American storekeeper of the neighboring town, who had come to the meeting to see what was going on, and had been interrupting the speaker with many rude remarks; and when Stanley, in his immaculate suit of gray check, his gray spats, and his eyeglass, passed by where he was sitting, it seemed as if all his slumbering hatred for England burst at once into flame!

"My word!" he mimicked, "'ere's a rum 'un—somebody should warn the Kaiser! It's not fair to take the poor man unawares—here is some of the real old English fighting-stock."

Stanley turned in surprise and looked his tormentor in the face. His look of insipid good-nature lured the German on.

"That is what is wrong with the British Empire," he jeered; "there are too many of these underbred aristocrats, all pedigree and no brains, like the long-nosed collies. God help them when they meet the Germans—that is all I have to say!"

He was quite right in his last sentence—that was all he had to say. It was his last word for the evening, and it looked as if it might be his last word for an indefinite time, for the unexpected happened.

Psychologists can perhaps explain it. We cannot. Stanley, who like charity had borne all things, endured all things, believed all things, suddenly became a new creature, a creature of rage, blind, consuming, terrible! You have heard of the worm turning? This was a case of a worm turning into a tank!

People who were there said that Stanley seemed to grow taller, his eyes glowed, his chin grew firm, his shoulders ceased to be apologetic. He whirled upon the German and landed a blow on his jaw that sounded like a blow-out! Before any one could speak, it was followed by another and the German lay on the floor!

Then Stanley turned to the astonished audience and delivered the most successful recruiting speech that had ever been given in the Pembina Valley.

"You have sat here all evening," he cried, "and have listened to this miserable hound insulting your country—this man who came here a few years ago without a cent and now has made a fortune in Canada, and I have no doubt is now conspiring with Canada's enemies, and would betray us into the hands of those enemies if he could. For this man I have the hatred which one feels for an enemy, but for you Canadians who have sat here and swallowed his insults, I have nothing but contempt. This man belongs to the race of people who cut hands off children, and outrage women; and now, when our Empire calls for men to go out and stop these devilish things, you sit here and let this traitor insult your country. You are all braver than I am, too; I am only a joke to most of you, a freak, a looney,—you have said so,—but I won't stand for this."

That night recruiting began in the valley and Stanley was the first man to sign on. The recruiting agent felt that it was impossible to turn down a man who had shown so much fighting spirit; and, besides, he was a small man and he had a face which he prized highly!

When the boys of the valley went to Valcartier there was none among them who had more boxes of home-made candy or more pairs of socks than Stanley; nor was any woman prouder of her boy than Mrs. Corbett was of the lad she had taken into her home and into her heart ten years before.

They were sent overseas almost at once, and, after a short training in England, went at once to the firing-line.

It was a dull, foggy morning, and although it was quite late the street-lamps were still burning, and while they could not make much impression on the darkness, at least they made a luminous top on the lamp-posts and served as a guide to the travelers who made their way into the city. In the breakfast-room of Mayflower Lodge it was dark, and gloomier still, for "the master" was always in his worst mood in the morning, and on this particular morning his temper was aggravated by the presence of his wife's mother and two sisters from Leith, who always made him envious of the men who marry orphans, who are also the last of their race.

Mr. Goodman was discussing the war-situation, and abusing the Government in that peculiarly bitter way of the British patriot.

His wife, a faded, subdued little woman, sat opposite him and contributed to the conversation twittering little broken phrases of assent. Her life had been made up of scenes like this. She was of the sweet and pliable type, which, with the best intentions in the world, has made life hard for other women.

Mr. Goodman gradually worked back to his old grievance.

"This is a time for every man to do his bit, and here am I too old to go and with no son to represent me—I who came from a family of six sons! Anyway, why doesn't the Government pass conscription and drag out the slackers who lounge in the parks and crowd the theaters?"

Aunt Louisa paused in the act of helping herself to marmalade and regarded him with great displeasure; then cried shrilly:—

"Now, Arthur, that is nothing short of treason, for I tell you we will not allow our dear boys to be taken away like galley-slaves; I tell you Britons never, never shall be slaves, and I for one will never let my Bertie go—his young life is too precious to be thrown away. I spent too many nights nursing him through every infantile disease—measles, whooping-cough,—you know yourself, my dear Clara,—beside the times that he broke his arm and his leg; though I still think that the cold compress is the best for a delicate constitution, and I actually ordered the doctor out of the house—"

55

"What has that to do with conscription?" asked her brother-in-law gruffly. "I tell you it is coming and no one will be gladder than I am."

"I think it is nothing short of unkind the way that you have been speaking of the Germans. I know I never got muffins like the muffins I got in Berlin that time; and, anyway, there are plenty of the commoner people to go to fight, and they have such large families that they will not miss one as I would miss my Bertie, and he has just recently become engaged to such a dear girl! In our home we simply try to forget this stupid war, but when I come here I hear nothing else—I wonder how you stand it, dear Clara."

Aunt Louisa here dabbed her eyes with her handkerchief in a way that her brother-in-law particularly detested.

"You will hear more about the war some of these days," he said, "when a German Zeppelin drops bombs on London."

Aunt Louisa came as near snorting as a well-bred lady could come, so great was her disdain at this suggestion.

"Zeppelin!" she said scornfully—"on England!! You forget, sir, that we are living in a civilized age! Zeppelin! Indeed, and who would let them, I wonder! I am surprised at you, sir, and so is mother, although she has not spoken."

"You will probably be more surprised before long; life is full of surprises these days."

Just then the butler brought him a wire, the contents of which seemed to bear out this theory, for it told him that Private Stanley Goodman, of the First Canadian Battalion, for conspicuous bravery under fire had been recommended for the D.C.M., but regretted to inform him that Private Goodman had been seriously wounded and was now in the Third Canadian Hospital, Flanders.

The nursing sister, accustomed to strange sights, wondered why this wounded man was so cold, and then she noticed that he had not on his overcoat, and she asked him why he was not wearing it on such a bitter cold night as this. In spite of all his efforts his teeth chattered as he tried to answer her.

"I had to leave a dead friend of mine on the field to-night," said Stanley, speaking with difficulty. "And I could not leave him there with the rain falling on him, could I, sister? It seemed hard to have to leave him, anyway, but we got all the wounded in."

In twenty-four hours after they received the telegram his father and mother stood by his bedside. Only his eyes and his forehead could be seen, for the last bullet which struck him had ploughed its way through his cheek; the chin which had so offended his father's artistic eye—what was left of it—was entirely hidden by the bandage. The chill which he had taken, with the loss of blood, and the shock of a shrapnel wound in his side, made recovery impossible, the nurse said. While they stood beside the bed waiting for him to open his eyes, the nurse told them of his having taken off his coat to cover a dead comrade.

When at last Stanley opened his eyes, there was a broken and sorrowful old man, from whose spirit all the imperious pride had gone, kneeling by his bedside and humbly begging his forgiveness. On the other side of the bed his mother stood with a great joy in her faded face.

"Stanley—Stanley," sobbed his father, every reserve broken down; "I have just found you—and now how can I lose you so soon. Try to live for my sake, and let me show you how sorry I am."

Stanley's eyes showed the distress which filled his tender heart.

"Please don't, father," he said, speaking with difficulty; "I am only very happy—indeed, quite jolly. But you mustn't feel sorry, father—I have been quite a duffer! thanks awfully for all you have done for me—I know how disappointed you were in me—I did want to make good for your sakes and it is a bit rough that now—I should be obliged—to die.... But it is best to go while the going is good—isn't it, sir? It's all a beautiful dream—to me—and it does seem—so jolly—to have you both here."

He lay still for a long time; then, rousing himself, said, "I'm afraid I have been dreaming again—no, this is father; you are sure, sir, are you?—about the medal and all that—and this is mother, is it?—it is all quite like going home—I am so happy; it seems as if permission had come."

He laughed softly behind his bandages, a queer, little, choking, happy laugh; and there, with his mother's arms around him, while his father, stern no longer, but tender and loving, held his hand, "permission" came and the homesick, hungry heart of the boy entered into rest.

CHAPTER IX
THE SLACKER—IN UNIFORM

Mrs. P.A. Brunton was convinced that she was an exceptional woman in every way. She would tell you this in the first fifteen minutes of conversation that you had with her, for many of her sentences began, "Now, I know, of course, that I am peculiar in many ways"; or, "I am afraid you will not understand me when I say this"; or, "I am afraid I am hopelessly old-fashioned in this." She would explain with painstaking elaboration that she did not know why she was so peculiar, but her manner indicated that she was quite content to be so; indeed, it can only be described as one of boastful resignation. She seemed to glory in her infirmity.

Mrs. Brunton was quite opposed to women voting, and often spoke with sorrow of the movement, which to her meant the breaking-up of the home and all its sacred traditions. She did not specify how this would be done, but her attitude toward all new movements was one of keen distrust. She often said that of course she would be able to vote intelligently, for she had had many advantages and had listened to discussions of public matters all her life, having been brought up in an atmosphere of advanced thinking; but she realized that her case was an exceptional one. It was not the good fortune of every woman to have had a college course as she had, and she really could not see what good could come from a movement which aimed at making all women equal! Why, if women ever got the vote, an ignorant washwoman's vote might kill hers! It was so much better to let women go on as they were going, exerting their indirect influence; and then it was the woman of wealth and social prestige who was able to exert this influence, just as it should be! She certainly did not crave a vote, and would do all she could to prevent other women from getting it.

Mrs. Brunton had come from the East, and although she had lived many years in the West, she could never forget what a sacrifice she had made by coming to a new country. Being a college graduate, too, seemed to be something she could not outgrow!

When her only boy was old enough to go to school, she became the teacher's bad dream, for she wrote many notes and paid many calls to explain that Garth was not at all like other children and must not be subjected to the same discipline as they, for he had a proud and haughty spirit that would not submit to discipline unless it were tactfully disguised. Garth was a quiet, mild little lad who would have been much like other boys if left alone.

Garth was twenty years old when the war began, and he was then attending the university. He first spoke of enlisting when the war had gone on a year.

"Enlist!" his mother cried, when he mentioned it to her, "I should say not—you are my only child, and I certainly did not raise you to be a soldier. There are plenty of common people to do the fighting; there are men who really like it; but I have other ambitions for you—you are to be a university man."

When the Third University Company went, he spoke of it again, but his mother held firm.

"Do you think I am going to have you sleeping in those awful trenches, with every Tom, Dick, and Harry? I tell you soldiering is a rough business, and I cannot let a boy of mine go—a boy who has had your advantages must not think of it."

"But, mother, there are lots of boys going who have had just as good advantages as I have."

Just then came in Emily Miller, the little girl from next door whose brother was going away the next day. Emily was an outspoken young lady of fourteen.

"When are you going, Garth?" she asked pointedly.

"He is not going," said his mother firmly. "His duty is at home finishing his education, and I am simply amazed at your mother for letting Robert go. Does she not believe in education? Of course I know there are not many who lay the stress on it that I do, but with me it is education first—always."

"But the war won't wait," said Emily; "my mother would be very glad to have Bob finish his education, but she's afraid it will be over then."

"War or no war, I say let the boys get their education—what is life without it?"

Emily surveyed her calmly, and then said, "What would happen to us if every mother held her boy back—what if every mother took your attitude, Mrs. Brunton?"

"You need not speculate on that, child, for they won't. Most mothers run with the popular fancy—they go with the crowd—never thinking, but I have always been peculiar, I know."

"Oh, mother, cut out that 'peculiar' business—it makes me tired!" said Garth undutifully.

When Robert Miller came in to say good-bye, he said: "You'll be lonesome, Garth, when we all go and you are left with the women and the old men—but perhaps you will enjoy being the only young man at the party."

"Garth may go later," said his mother,—"at least if the war lasts long enough,—but not as a private. I will not object to his taking the officers' classes at the university."

"See, Bob," crowed Garth, "I'll have you and Jim Spaulding for my two batmen over there. But never mind, I'll be good to you and will see that you get your ha'pennyworth of 'baccy and mug of beer regular."

Mrs. Brunton laughed delightedly. "Garth always sees the funny side," she cooed.

"That certainly is a funny side all right," said Robert, "but he'll never see it! These pasteboard officers never last after they get over—they can only carry it off here. Over there, promotions are on merit, not on political pull."

The third, fourth, and fifth contingents went from the university, and still Garth pursued the quest of learning. His mother openly rebuked the mothers of the boys who had gone. "Let the man on the street go! Look at the unemployed men on our streets!" she said; "why aren't they made to go—and leave our university boys at home?"

"Every man owes a duty to his country," one of the mothers said. "If one man neglects or refuses to pay, that is no reason for others to do the same. This is a holy war—holier than any of the crusades—for the crusader went out to restore the tomb of our Lord, and that is only a material thing; but our boys are going out to give back to the world our Lord's ideals, and I know they are more precious to Him than any tomb could be!"

"My dear Mrs. Mason," said Garth's mother, "you are simply war-mad like so many women—it is impossible to reason with you."

A year went by, and many of the university boys were wounded and some were killed. To the mothers of these went Mrs. Brunton with words of sympathy, but came away wondering. Some way they did not seem to receive her warmly.

"Where is Garth now?" asked one of these women.

"He's thinking of taking the officers' training," answered Mrs. Brunton, "as soon as the college term closes. A boy meets the very nicest people there, and I do think that is so important, to meet nice people."

"And no Germans!" said the other woman tartly.

Mrs. Brunton gave a very select and intellectual farewell party for Garth when he went to another city to take the officers' training, and she referred to him as "my brave soldier laddie," much to the amusement of some of the party.

In two weeks he came home on leave of absence, very elegant in his new uniform. He also brought cabinet-sized photographs which cost eighteen dollars a dozen. Another party was held—the newspaper said he was the "*raison d'être* for many pleasant social gatherings."

At the end of two weeks he went out again to take more classes. He was very popular with the girls, and the mother of one of them came to visit Mrs. Brunton. They agreed on the subject of military training and education, and exceptional women, and all was gay and happy.

At the end of three months Garth again came home. No hero from the scenes of battle was ever more royally received, and an afternoon reception was held, when patriotic songs were sung and an uncle of the young man made a speech.

Soon after that Garth went to Toronto and took another course, because his mother thought it was only right for him to see his own country first, before going abroad; and, besides, no commission had yet been offered him. The short-sightedness of those in authority was a subject which Mrs. Brunton often dwelt on, but she said she could not help being glad.

Meanwhile the war went wearily on; battalion after battalion went out and scattering remnants came home. Empty sleeves, rolled trousers legs, eyes that stared, and heads that rolled pitifully appeared on the streets. On the sunshiny afternoons many of these broken men sat on the verandas of the Convalescent Home and admired the smart young lieutenant who went whistling by—and wondered what force he was with.

The war went on to the completion of its third year. Garth had attended classes in three cities, and had traveled Canada from end to end. There had been four farewell parties and three receptions in his honor. He came home again for what his mother termed "a well-earned rest."

He sat on the veranda one day luxuriously ensconced in a wicker chair, smoking a cigarette whose blue wreaths of smoke he blew gayly from him. He was waiting for the postman—one of Mae's letters had evidently gone astray, and the postman, who seemed to be a stupid fellow, had probably given it to some one else. He had made several mistakes lately, and Garth determined that it was time he was reprimanded—the young officer would attend to that.

"Posty" came at last, a few minutes late again, and Garth rapped imperiously with his cane, as "Posty," peering at the addresses of the letters, came up the steps.

"See here," cried Garth, "let me see what you have!"

61

"Posty" started nervously and the letters dropped from his hands. While he gathered them up, Garth in his most military manner delivered himself of a caustic rebuke:—

"You have left letters here which belong elsewhere, and I have lost letters through your carelessness. What is the matter with you anyway— can't you read?" he snapped.

"Yes, sir," stammered "Posty," flushing as red as the band on his hat.

"Well, then," went on the young officer, "why don't you use your eyes—where do you keep them anyway?"

"Posty" stood at attention as he answered with measured deliberation:—

"I have one of them here ... but I left the other one at Saint-Éloi. Were you thinking of hunting it up for me, sir,—when—you—go—over?"

That was six weeks ago. Still the war goes on. Returned men walk our streets, new pale faces lie on hospital pillows, telegraph boys on wheels carry dread messages to the soldiers' homes.

Garth has gone back to an Eastern city for another course (this time in signaling). He gave a whole set of buttons off his uniform to Mae before he went—and he had his photograph taken again!

Even if he does not get over in time to do much in this war, it is worth something to have such a perfectly trained young officer ready for the next war!

CHAPTER X
NATIONAL SERVICE—ONE WAY

There are some phrases in our conversations now that are used so often that they seem to be in some danger of losing their meaning. The snap goes out of them by too much handling, like an elastic band which has been stretched too far. One of these is "national service."

If the work of the soldier, who leaves home, position, and safety behind him, and goes forth to meet hardship and danger, receiving as recompense one dollar and ten cents per day, is taken as the standard of comparison, the question of national service becomes very simple, indeed, for there is but one class, and no other that is even distantly related to it, but if national service is taken to mean the doing of something for our country's good which we would not feel it our duty to do but for the emergencies created by the war, then there are many ways in which the sincere citizen may serve.

The Abilene Valley School was closed all last year, and weeds are growing in the garden in which the year before flowers and vegetables, scarlet runners and cabbages, poppies and carrots, had mingled in wild profusion. The art-muslin curtains are draggled and yellow, and some of the windows, by that strange fate which overtakes the windows in unoccupied houses, are broken.

The school was not closed for lack of children. Not at all. Peter Rogowski, who lives a mile east, has seven children of school-age himself, from bright-eyed Polly aged fourteen to Olga aged six, and Mr. Rogowski is merely one of the neighbors in this growing settlement, where large families are still to be found. There are twenty-four children of school-age in the district, and in 1915, when Mr. Ellis taught there, the average attendance was nineteen. At the end of the term Mr. Ellis, who was a university student, abandoned his studies and took his place in the ranks of the Army Medical Corps, and is now nursing wounded men in France. He said that it would be easy to find some one else to take the school. He was thinking of the droves of teachers who had attended the Normal with him. There seemed to be no end of them, but apparently there was, for in the year that followed there were more than one hundred and fifty schools closed because no teacher could be found.

After waiting a whole year for a teacher to come, Polly Rogowski, as the spring of 1917 opened, declared her intention of going to Edmonton to find work and go to school. Polly's mother upheld her in this determination, and together they scraped up enough money to pay her railway fare, and board for one week, although it took all that they had been putting away to get Mrs. Rogowski's teeth fixed. But Polly's mother knew that when her Polly began to teach there would be money and plenty for things like that, and anyway they had not ached so bad for a while.

The city, even Edmonton, is a fearsome place for a fourteen-year-old girl who has no friends, seven dollars in money, and only an intense desire for an education to guide her through its devious ways. But the first night that Polly was away, her mother said an extra prayer before the

Blessed Virgin, who, being a mother herself, would understand how much a young girl in a big city needs special care.

It was a cold, dark day when Polly with her small pack arrived at the C.N.R. Station, and looked around her. Surely no crusader going forth to restore the tomb of his Lord ever showed more courage than black-eyed Polly when she set forth on this lonely pilgrimage to find learning. She had heard of the danger of picking up with strangers, and the awful barred windows behind which young girls languished and died, and so refused to answer when the Travelers' Aid of the Y.W.C.A. in friendliest tones asked if she might help her.

Polly was not to be deceived by friendly tones. The friendly ones were the worst! She held her head high and walked straight ahead, just as if she knew where she was going. Polly had a plan of action. She was going to walk on and on until she came to a house marked in big letters "BOARDING-HOUSE," and she would go in there and tell the lady that she wanted to get a room for one day, and then she would leave her bundle and go out and find a school and see the teacher. Teachers were all good men and would help you! Then she would find a place where they wanted a girl to mind a baby or wash dishes, or maybe milk a cow; and perhaps she would have a bed all to herself. City houses were so big and had so many rooms, and she had heard that in some of the beds only one person slept! Having her programme so well laid out, it is no wonder that she refused to confide in the blue serge lady who spoke to her.

Polly set off at a quick pace, looking straight ahead of her across the corner of the station yard, following the crowd. The Travelers' Aid followed close behind, determined to keep a close watch on the independent little Russian girl.

At the corner of First and Jasper, Polly stopped confused. A great crowd stood around the bulletin board and excitedly read the news of the Russian revolution; automobiles honked their horns, and street-cars clanged and newsboys shouted, and more people than Polly had ever seen before surged by her. For the first time Polly's stout heart failed her. She had not thought it would be quite like this!

Turning round, she was glad to see the woman who had spoken to her at the station. In this great bustling, pushing throng she seemed like an old friend.

"Do you know where I could find a boarding-house?" asked Polly breathlessly.

The Travelers' Aid took her by the hand and piloted her safely across the street; and when the street-car had clanged by and she could be heard, she told Polly that she would take her to a boarding-house where she would be quite safe.

Polly stopped and asked her what was the name of the place.

"Y.W.C.A.," said the Aid, smiling.

Polly gave a sigh of relief. "I know what that is," she said. "Mr. Ellis said that was the place to go when you go to a city. Will you let me stay until I find a school?"

"We'll find the school," said the other woman. "That is what we are for; we look after girls like you. We are glad to find a girl who wants to go to school."

Polly laid her pack down to change hands and looked about her in delight. The big brick buildings, the store-windows, even the street-signs with their flaring colors, were all beautiful to her.

"Gee!" she said, "I like the city—it's swell!"

Polly was taken to the office of the secretary of the Y.W.C.A., and there, under the melting influence of Miss Bradshaw's kind eyes and sweet voice, she told all her hopes and fears.

"Our teacher has gone to be a soldier and we could not get another, for they say it is too lonesome—out our way—and how can it be lonesome? There's children in every house. But, anyway, lady-teachers won't come and the men are all gone to the war. I'll bet I won't be scared to teach when I grow up, but of course I won't be a lady; it's different with them—they are always scared of something. We have a cabin for the teacher, and three chairs and a painted table and a stove and a bed, and a brass knob on the door, and we always brought cream and eggs and bread for the teacher; and we washed his dishes for him, and the girl that had the best marks all week could scrub his floor on Friday afternoons. He was so nice to us all that we all cried when he enlisted, but he explained it all to us—that there are some things dearer than life and he just felt that he had to go. He said that he would come back if he was not killed. Maybe he will only have one arm and one leg, but we won't mind as long as there is enough of him to come back. We tried and tried to get another teacher, but there are not enough to fill the good schools, and ours is twenty miles from a station and in a foreign settlement.... I'm foreign, too," she added honestly; "I'm Russian."

"The Russians are our allies," said the secretary, "and you are a real little Canadian now, Polly, and you are not a bit foreign. I was born in Tipperary myself, and that is far away from Canada, too."

"Oh, yes, I know about it being a long way there," Polly said. "But that doesn't matter, it is the language that counts. You see my mother can't talk very good English and that is what makes us foreign, but she wants us all to know English, and that is why she let me come away, and I will do all I can to learn, and I will be a teacher some day, and then I will go back and plant the garden and she will send me butter, for I will live in the cabin. But it is too bad that we cannot have a teacher to come to us, for now, when I am away, there is no one to teach my mother English, for Mary does not speak the English well by me, and the other children will soon forget it if we cannot get a teacher."

While she was speaking, the genial secretary was doing some hard thinking. This little messenger from the up-country had carried her message right into the heart of one woman, one who was accustomed to carry her impulses into action.

The Local Council of Women of the City of Edmonton met the next day in the club-room of the Y.W.C.A., and it was a well-attended meeting, for the subject to be discussed was that of "National Service for Women." As the time drew near for the meeting to begin, it became evident that great interest was being taken in the subject, for the room was full, and animated discussions were going on in every corner. This was not the first meeting that had been held on this subject, and considerable indignation was heard that no notice had been taken by the Government of the request that had been sent in some months previous, asking that women be registered for national service as well as men.

"They never even replied to our suggestion," one woman said. "You would have thought that common politeness would have prompted a reply. It was a very civil note that we sent—I wrote it myself."

"Hush! Don't be hard on the Government," said an older woman, looking up from her knitting. "They have their own troubles—think of Quebec! And then you know women's work is always taken for granted; they know we will do our bit without being listed or counted."

"But I want to do something else besides knitting," the first speaker said; "it could be done better and cheaper anyway by machinery, and that would set a lot of workers free. Why don't we register ourselves, all of us who mean business? This is our country, and if the Government is asleep at the switch, that is no reason why we should be. I tell you I am for conscription for every man and woman."

"Well, suppose we all go with you and sign up—name, age, present address; married?—if so, how often?—and all that sort of thing; what will you do with us, then?" asked Miss Wheatly, who was just back from the East where she had been taking a course in art. "I am tired of having my feelings all wrought upon and then have to settle down to knitting a dull gray sock or the easy task of collecting Red Cross funds from perfectly willing people who ask me to come in while they make me a cup of tea. I feel like a real slacker, for I have never yet done a hard thing. I did not let any one belonging to me go, for the fairly good reason that I have no male relatives; I give money, but I have never yet done without a meal or a new pair of boots when I wanted them. There is no use of talking of putting me to work on a farm, for no farmer would be bothered with me for a minute, and the farmer's wife has trouble enough now without giving her the care of a greenhorn like me—why, I would not know when a hen wanted to set!"

"You do not need to know," laughed the conscriptionist; "the hen will attend to that without any help from you; and, anyway, we use incubators now and the hen is exempt from all family cares—she can have a Career if she wants to."

"I am in earnest about this," Miss Wheatly declared; "I am tired of this eternal talk of national service and nothing coming of it. Now, if any of you know of a hard, full-sized woman's job that I can do, you may lead me to it!"

Then the meeting began. There was a very enthusiastic speaker who told of the great gift that Canada had given to the Empire, the gift of men and wheat, bread and blood—the sacrament of empire. She then told of what a sacrifice the men make who go to the front, who lay their young lives down for their country and do it all so cheerfully. "And now," she said, "what about those of us who stay at home, who have three good meals every day, who sleep in comfortable beds and have not departed in any way from our old comfortable way of living. Wouldn't you like to do something to help win the war?"

There was a loud burst of applause here, but Miss Wheatly sat with a heavy frown on her face.

"Wasn't that a perfectly wonderful speech?" the secretary whispered to her when the speaker had finished with a ringing verse of poetry all about sacrifice and duty.

"It is all the same old bunk," Miss Wheatly said bitterly; "I often wonder how they can speak so long and not make one practical suggestion. Wouldn't you like to help win the war? That sounds so foolish—of course we would like to win the war. It is like the old-fashioned evangelists who used to say, 'All who would like to go to heaven will please stand up.' Everybody stood, naturally."

While they were whispering, they missed the announcement that the president was making, which was that there was a young girl from the North Country who had come to the meeting and wished to say a few words. There was a deep, waiting silence, and then a small voice began to speak. It was Miss Polly Rogowski from the Abilene Valley District.

There was no fear in Polly's heart—she was not afraid of anything. Not being a lady, of course, and having no reputation to sustain, and being possessed with one thought, and complete master of it, her speech had true eloquence. She was so small that the women at the back of the room had to stand up to see her.

"I live at Abilene Valley and there are lots of us. I am fourteen years old and Mary is twelve, and Annie is eleven, and Mike is ten, and Peter is nine, and Ivan is seven, and Olga is six, and that is all we have old enough to go to school; but there are lots more of other children in our neighborhood, but our teacher has gone away to the war and we cannot get another one, for lady-teachers are all too scared, but I don't think they would be if they would only come, for we will chop the wood, and one of us will stay at night and sleep on the floor, and we will light the fires and get the breakfast, and we bring eggs and cream and everything like that, and we could give the teacher a cat and a dog; and the girl that had done the best work all week always got to scrub the floor when our last teacher was there; and we had a nice garden—and flowers, and now there is not anything, and the small children are forgetting what Mr. Ellis taught them; for our school has been closed all last summer, and sometimes Peter and Ivan and the other little boys go over to the cabin and look in at the windows, and it is all so quiet and sad—they cry."

There was a stricken silence in the room which Polly mistook for a lack of interest and redoubled her efforts.

"We have twenty-four children altogether and they are all wanting a teacher to come. I came here to go to school, but if I can get a teacher to go back with me, I will go back. I thought I would try to learn quick and go back then, but when I saw all so many women able to read right off, and all looking so smart at learning, I thought I would ask you if one of you would please come. We give our teacher sixty-five dollars a month, and when you want to come home we will bring you to the station—it is only twenty miles—and the river is not deep only when it rains, and then even I know how to get through and not get in the holes; and if you will come we must go to-morrow, for the ice is getting rotten in the river and won't stand much sun."

That was the appeal of the country to the city; of the foreign-born to the native-born; of the child to the woman.

The first person to move was Miss Wheatly, who rose quietly and walked to the front of the room and faced the audience. "Madam President," she began in her even voice, "I have been waiting quite a while for this, I think. I said to-day that if any one knew of a real, full-sized woman's job, I would like to be led to it.... Well—it seems that I have been led"

She then turned to Polly and said, "I can read right off and am not afraid, not even of the river, if you promise to keep me out of the holes, and I believe I can find enough of a diploma to satisfy the department, and as you have heard the river won't stand much sun, so you will kindly notice that my address has changed to Abilene Valley Post-Office."

Polly held her firmly by the hand and they moved toward the door. Polly turned just as they were passing through the door and made her quaint and graceful curtsy, saying, "I am glad I came, and I guess we will be for going now."

CHAPTER XI
THE ORPHAN

Just a little white-faced lad Sitting on the "Shelter" floor; Eyes which seemed so big and sad, Watched me as I passed the door. Turning back, I tried to win From that sober face a smile With some foolish, trifling thing, Such as children's hearts beguile.

But the look which shot me through Said as plain as speech could be: "Life has been all right for you! But it is no joke for me! I'm not big enough to know— And I wonder, wonder why My dear 'Daddy' had to go And my mother had to die!

"You've a father, I suppose? And a mother—maybe—too? You can laugh and joke at life? It has been all right for you? Spin your top, and wave your fan! You've a home and folks who care Laugh about it those who can! Joke about it—those who dare —But excuse me—if I'm glum I can't bluff it off—like some!"

Then I sadly came away And felt guilty, all the day!

Dr. Frederick Winters was a great believer in personal liberty for every one—except, of course, the members of his own family. For them he craved every good thing except this. He was kind, thoughtful, courteous, and generous—a beneficent despot.

There is much to be said in favor of despotic government after all. It is so easy of operation; it is so simple and direct—one brain, one will, one law, with no foolish back-talk, bickerings, murmurings, mutinies, letters to the paper. A democracy has it beaten, of course, on the basis of liberty, but there is much to be said in favor of an autocracy in the matter of efficiency.

"King Asa did that which was right in the sight of the Lord"; and in his reign the people were happy and contented and had no political differences. There being only one party, the "Asaites," there were no partisan newspapers, no divided homes, no mixed marriages, as we have to-day when Liberals and Conservatives, disregarding the command to be not unequally yoked together, marry. All these distressing circumstances were eliminated in good King Asa's reign.

It is always a mistake to pursue a theory too far. When we turn the next page of the sacred story we read that King Omri, with the same powers as King Asa had had, turned them to evil account and oppressed the people in many ways and got himself terribly disliked. Despotism seems to work well or ill according to the despot, and so, as a form of government, it has steadily declined in favor.

Despotic measures have thriven better in homes than in states. Homes are guarded by a wall of privacy, a delicate distaste for publicity, a shrinking from all notoriety such as rebellion must inevitably bring, and for this reason the weaker ones often practice a peace-at-any-price policy, thinking of the alert eyes that may be peering through the filet lace of the window across the street.

Mrs. Winters submitted to the despotic rule of Dr. Winters for no such reason as this. She submitted because she liked it, and because she did not know that it was despotic. It saved her the exertion of making decisions for herself, and her conscience was always quite clear. "The Doctor will not let me," she had told the women when they had asked her to play for the Sunday services at the mission. "The Doctor thought it was too cold for me to go out," had been her explanation when on one occasion she had failed to appear at a concert where she had promised to play the accompaniments; and in time people ceased to ask her to do anything, her promises were so likely to be broken.

When the Suffrage agitators went to see her and tried to show her that she needed a vote, she answered all their arguments by saying, "I have such a good husband that these arguments do not apply to me at all"; and all their talk about spiritual independence and personal responsibility fell on very pretty, but very deaf, ears. The women said she was a hopeless case.

"I wonder," said one of the women afterwards in discussing her, "when Mrs. Winters presents herself at the heavenly gate and there is asked what she has done to make the world better, and when she has to confess that she has never done anything outside of her own house, and nothing there except agreeable things, such as entertaining friends who next week will entertain her, and embroidering 'insets' for corset-covers for dainty ladies who already have corset-covers enough to fill a store-window,—I wonder if she will be able to put it over on the heavenly doorkeeper that 'the Doctor would not let her.' If all I hear is true, Saint Peter will say, 'Who is this person you call the Doctor?' and when she explains that the Doctor was her husband, Saint Peter will say, 'Sorry, lady, we cannot recognize marriage relations here at all—it is unconstitutional, you know—there is no marrying or giving in marriage after you cross the Celestial Meridian. I turned back a woman this morning who handed in the same excuse—there seems to have been a good deal of this business of one person's doing the thinking for another on earth, but we can't stand for it here. I'm sorry, lady, but I can't let you in—it would be as much as my job is worth.'"

Upon this happy household, as upon some others not so happy, came the war!—and Dr. Winters's heroic soul responded to the trumpet's call. He was among the first to present himself for active service in the Overseas Force. When he came home and told his wife, she got the first shock of her life. It was right, of course, it must be right, but he should have told her, and she remonstrated with him for the first time in her life. Why had he not consulted her, she asked, before taking such a vital step? Then Dr. Winters expressed in words one of the underlying principles of his life. "A man's first duty is to his country and his God," he said, "and even if you had objected, it would not have changed my decision."

Mrs. Winters looked at him in surprise. "But, Frederick," she cried, "I have never had any authority but you. I have broken promises when you told me to, disappointed people, disappointed myself, but never complained—thinking in a vague way that you would do the same for me if I asked you to—your word was my law. What would you think if I volunteered for a nurse without asking you—and then told you my country's voice sounded clear and plain above all others?"

"It is altogether different," he said brusquely. "The country's business concerns men, not women. Woman's place is to look after the homes of the nation and rear children. Men are concerned with the big things of life."

71

Mrs. Winters looked at him with a new expression on her face. "I have fallen down, then," she said, "on one part of my job—I have brought into the world and cared for no children. All my life—and I am now forty years of age—has been given to making a home pleasant for one man. I have been a housekeeper and companion for one person. It doesn't look exactly like a grown woman's whole life-work, now, does it?"

"Don't talk foolishly, Nettie," he said; "you suit me."

"That's it," she said quickly; "I suit you—but I do not suit the church women, the Civic Club women, the Hospital Aid women, the Children's Shelter women; they call me a slacker, and I am beginning to think I am."

"I would like to know what they have to do with it?" he said hotly; "you are my wife and I am the person concerned."

Without noticing what he said, she continued: "Once I wanted to adopt a baby, you remember, when one of your patients died, and I would have loved to do it; but you said you must not be disturbed at night and I submitted. Still, if it had been our own, you would have had to be disturbed and put up with it like other people, and so I let you rule me. I have never had any opinion of my own."

"Nettie, you are excited," he said gently; "you are upset, poor girl, about my going away—I don't wonder. Come out with me; I am going to speak at a recruiting meeting."

Her first impulse was to refuse, for there were many things she wanted to think out, but the habit of years was on her and she went.

The meeting was a great success. It was the first days of the war, when enthusiasm seethed and the little town throbbed with excitement. The news was coming through of the destruction and violation of Belgium; the women wept and men's faces grew white with rage.

Dr. Winters's fine face was alight with enthusiasm as he spoke of the debt that every man now owes to his country. Every man who is able to hold a gun, he said, must come to the help of civilization against barbarism. These dreadful outrages are happening thousands of miles away, but that makes them none the less real. Humanity is being attacked by a bully, a ruffian,—how can any man stay at home? Let no consideration of family life keep you from doing your duty. Every human being must give an account of himself to God. What did you do in the great day of testing? will be the question asked you in that great day of reckoning to which we are all coming.

When he was through speaking, amid the thunderous applause, five young men walked down to the front and signified their intention of going.

72

"Why, that's Willie Shepherd, and he is his mother's only support," whispered one of the women; "I don't think he should go."

When they went home that night Mrs. Winters told the Doctor what she had heard the women say, and even added her remonstrance too.

"This is no time for remonstrance," he had cried; "his mother will get along; the Patriotic Fund will look after her. I tell you human relationships are forgotten in this struggle! We must save our country. One broken heart more or less cannot be taken into consideration. Personal comfort must not be thought of. There is only one limit to service and sacrifice, and that is capacity."

Every night after that he addressed meetings, and every night recruits came to the colors. His speeches vibrated with the spirit of sacrifice and the glory of service, and thrilled every heart that listened, and no heart was more touched than that of his wife, who felt that no future in the world would be so happy as to go and care for the wounded men.

She made the suggestion one night, and was quite surprised to find that the Doctor regarded it favorably. All that night she lay awake from sheer joy: at last she was going to be of service—she was going to do something. She tried to tell herself of the hardships of the life, but nothing could dim her enthusiasm. "I hope it will be hard," she cried happily. "I want it hard to make up for the easy, idle years I have spent. I hate the ease and comfort and selfishness in which I have lived."

The next day her application went in and she began to attend the ambulance classes which were given in the little city by the doctors and nurses.

The Doctor was away so much that she was practically free to go and come as she liked, and the breath of liberty was sweet to her. She also saw, with further pangs of conscience, the sacrifices which other women were making. The Red Cross women seemed to work unceasingly.

The President of the Red Cross came to her office every morning at nine, and stayed till five.

"What about lunch?" Mrs. Winters asked her, one day. "Do you go home?"

"Oh, no," said the other woman; "I go out and get a sandwich."

"But I mean—what about your husband's lunch?"

"He goes home," the president said, "and sees after the children when they come in from school—of course I have a maid, you know."

"But doesn't he miss you dreadfully?" asked Mrs. Winters.

"Yes, I think he does, but not any more than the poor fellows in the trenches miss their wives. He is not able to go to the front himself and he is only too glad to leave me free to do all I can."

"But surely some other woman could be found," said Mrs. Winters, "who hasn't got as many family cares as you have."

"They could," said the president, "but they would probably tell you that their husbands like to have them at home—or some day would be stormy and they would 'phone down that 'Teddy' positively refused to let them come out. We have been busy people all our lives and have been accustomed to sacrifice and never feel a bit sorry for it—we've raised our six children and done without many things. It doesn't hurt us as it does the people who have always sat on cushioned seats. The Red Cross Society knows that it is a busy woman who can always find time to do a little more, and I am just as happy as can be doing this."

Mrs. Winters felt the unintentional rebuke in these words, and turned them over in her mind.

One day, three months after this, the Doctor told her that it was quite probable he would not be going overseas at all, for he was having such success recruiting that the major-general thought it advisable to have him go right on with it. "And so, Nettie," he said, "you had better cancel your application to go overseas, for of course, if I do not go, you will not."

For a moment she did not grasp what he meant. He spoke of it so casually. Not go! The thought of her present life of inactivity was never so repulsive. But silence fell upon her and she made no reply.

"We will not know definitely about it for a few weeks," he said, and went on reading.

After that, Mrs. Winters attended every recruiting meeting at which her husband spoke, eagerly memorizing his words, hardly knowing why, but she felt that she might need them. She had never been able to argue with any one—one adverse criticism of her position always caused her defense to collapse. So she collected all the material she could get on the subject of personal responsibility and sacrifice. Her husband's brilliant way of phrasing became a delight to her. But always, as she listened, vague doubts arose in her mind.

One day when she was sewing at the Red Cross rooms, the women were talking of a sad case that had occurred at the hospital. A soldier's wife had died, leaving a baby two weeks old and another little girl of four, who had been taken to the Children's Shelter, and who had cried so hard to be left with her mother. One of the women had been to see the sick woman the day before she died, and was telling the others about her.

"A dear little saint on earth she was—well bred, well educated, but without friends. Her only anxiety was for her children and sympathy for her husband. 'This will be sad news for poor Bob,' she said, 'but he'll know I did my best to live—I cannot get my breath—that's the worst—if I could only get my breath—I would abide the pain *some way*.' The baby is lovely, too,—a fine healthy boy. Now I wonder if there is any woman patriotic enough to adopt those two little ones whose mother is dead and whose father is in the trenches. The baby went to the Shelter yesterday."

"Of course they are well treated there," said Mrs. Winters.

"Well treated!" cried the president—"they are fed and kept warm and given all the care the matron and attendants can give them; but how can two or three women attend to twenty-five children? They do all they can, but it's a sad place just the same. I always cry when I see the mother-hungry look on their faces. They want to be owned and loved—they need some one belonging to them. Don't you know that settled look of loneliness? I call it the 'institutional face,' and I know it the minute I see it. Poor Bob Wilson—it will be sad news for him—he was our plumber and gave up a good job to go. At the station he kept saying to his wife to comfort her, for she was crying her heart out, poor girl, 'Don't cry, Minnie dear, I'm leaving you in good hands; they are not like strangers anymore, all these kind ladies; they'll see you through. Don't you remember what the Doctor said,'—that was your husband, Mrs. Winters,—'the women are the best soldiers of all—so you'll bear up, Minnie.'

"Minnie was a good soldier right enough," said the president, "but I wonder what Bob will think of the rest of us when he comes home—or doesn't come home. We let his Minnie die, and sent his two babies to the Children's Shelter. In this manner have we discharged our duty—we've taken it easy so far."

Mrs. Winters sat open-eyed, and as soon as she could, left the room. She went at once to the Shelter and asked to see the children.

Up the bare stairs, freshly scrubbed, she was taken, and into the day-nursery where many children sat on the floor, some idly playing with half-broken toys, one or two wailing softly, not as if they were looking for immediate returns, but just as a small protest against things in general. The little four-year-old girl, neatly dressed and smiling, came at once when the matron called her, and quickly said, "Will you take me to my mother? Am I going home now?"

"She asks every one that," the matron said aside.

"I have a little brother now," said the child proudly; "just down from heaven—we knew he was coming."

75

In one of the white cribs the little brother lay, in an embroidered quilt. The matron uncovered his face, and, opening one navy-blue eye, he smiled.

"He's a bonnie boy," the matron said; "he has slept ever since he came. But I cannot tell—somebody—I simply can't."

Mrs. Winters went home thinking so hard that she was afraid her husband would see the thoughts shining out, tell-tale, in her face.

She told him where she had been and was just leading up to the appeal which she had prepared, for the children, when a young man called to see the Doctor.

The young fellow had called for advice: his wife would not give her consent to his enlisting, and his heart was wrung with anxiety over what he should do.

The Doctor did not hesitate a minute. "Go right on," he said; "this is no time to let any one, however near and dear, turn us from our duty. We have ceased to exist as individuals—now we are a Nation and we must sacrifice the individual for the State. Your wife will come around to it and be glad that you were strong enough to do your duty. No person has any right to turn another from his duty, for we must all answer to Almighty God in this crisis, not to each other."

The next day, while the Doctor was away making a recruiting speech in another town, the delivery van of the leading furniture store stood at his back door and one high chair stood in it, one white crib was being put up-stairs in his wife's bedroom, and many foreign articles were in evidence in the room. The Swedish maid was all excitement and moved around on tip-toe, talking in a whisper.

"There ban coming a baby hare, and a li'l' girl. Gee! what will the Doctor man say! He ban quick enough to bring them other houses, no want none for self—oh, gee!"

Then she made sure that the key was not in the study door, for Olga was a student of human nature and wanted to get her information first-hand.

When the Doctor came in late that night, Mrs. Winters met him at the door as usual. So absorbed was he in telling her of the success of his meetings that he did not notice the excitement in her face.

"They came to-night in droves, Nettie," he said, as he drank the cocoa she had made for him.

"They can't help it, Fred," she declared enthusiastically, "when you put it to them the way you do. You are right, dear; it is not a time for any person to hold others back from doing what they see they should. It's a personal matter between us and God—we are not individuals any more—we are a state, and each man and woman must get under the burden. I hate this talk of 'business as usual'—I tell you it is nothing as usual."

He regarded her with surprise! Nettie had never made so long a speech before.

"It's your speeches, Fred; they are wonderful. Why, man alive, you have put backbone even into me—I who have been a jelly-fish all my life—and last night, when I heard you explain to that young fellow that he must not let his wife be his conscience, I got a sudden glimpse of things. You've been my conscience all my life, but, thank God, you've led me out into a clear place. I'm part of the State, and I am no slacker—I am going to do my bit. Come, Fred, I want to show you something."

He followed her without a word as she led the way to the room upstairs where two children slept sweetly.

"They are mine, Fred,—mine until the war is over, at least, and Private Wilson comes back; and if he does not come back, or if he will let me have them, they are mine forever."

He stared at this new woman, who looked like his wife.

"It was your last speech, Fred,—what you said to that young man. You told him to go ahead—his wife would come around, you said—she would see her selfishness. Then I saw a light shine on my pathway. Every speech has stiffened my backbone a little. I was like the mouse who timidly tiptoed out to the saucer of brandy, and, taking a sip, went more boldly back, then came again with considerable swagger; and at last took a good drink and then strutted up and down saying, 'Bring on your old black cat!' That's how I feel, Fred,—I'm going to be a mother to these two little children whose own mother has passed on and whose father is holding up the pillars of the Empire. It would hardly be fair to leave them to public charity, now, would it?"

"Well, Nettie," the Doctor said slowly, "I'll see that you do not attend any more recruiting meetings—you are too literal. But all the same," he said, "I am proud of my convert."

Olga Jasonjusen tiptoed gently away from the door, and going down the back stairs hugged herself gayly, saying, "All over—but the kissing. Oh, gee! He ain't too bad! He's just needed some one to cheek up to him. Bet she's sorry now she didn't sass him long ago."

CHAPTER XII
THE WAR-MOTHER

I saw my old train friend again. It was the day that one of our regiments went away, and we were all at the station to bid the boys good-bye.

The empty coaches stood on a siding, and the stream of khaki-clad men wound across the common from the Fair buildings, which were then used as a military camp. The men were heavily loaded with all their equipment, but cheerful as ever. The long-looked-for order to go forward had come at last!

Men in uniform look much the same, but the women who came with them and stood by them were from every station in life. There were two Ukrainian women, with colored shawls on their heads, who said good-bye to two of the best-looking boys in the regiment, their sons. It is no new thing for the Ukrainian people to fight for liberty! There were heavily veiled women, who alighted from their motors and silently watched the coaches filling with soldiers. Every word had been said, every farewell spoken; they were not the sort who say tempestuous good-byes, but their silence was like the silence of the open grave. There were many sad-faced women, wheeling go-carts, with children holding to their skirts crying loudly for "Daddy." There were tired, untidy women, overrun by circumstances, with that look about them which the Scotch call "through-other." There were many brave little boys and girls standing by their mothers, trying hard not to cry; there were many babies held up to the car-window to kiss a big brother or a father; there were the groups of chattering young people, with their boxes of candy and incessant fun; there were brides of a day, with their white-fox furs and new suits, and the great new sorrow in their eyes.

One fine-looking young giant made his way toward the train without speaking to any one, passing where a woman held her husband's hands, crying hysterically—we were trying to persuade her to let him go, for the conductor had given the first warning.

"I have no one to cry over me, thank God!" he said, "and I think I am the best off." But the bitterness in his tone belied his words.

"Then maybe I could pretend that you are my boy," said a woman's voice behind me, which sounded familiar; "you see I have no boy—now, and nobody to write to—and I just came down to-night to see if I could find one. I want to have some one belonging to me—even if they are going away!"

The young man laid down his bag and took her hand awkwardly. "I sure would be glad to oblige you," he said, "only I guess you could get one that was lots nicer. I am just a sort of a bo-hunk from the North Country."

"You'll do me," said the old lady, whom I recognized at once as my former train companion,—"you'll do me fine. Tell me your name and number, and I'll be your war-mother,—here's my card, I have it all ready,—I knew I'd get some one. Now, remember, I am your Next of Kin. Give in my name and I'll get the cable when you get the D.S.O., and I'll write to you every week and send you things. I just can't keep from sending parcels."

"Gee! This is sudden!" said the boy, laughing; "but it's nice!"

"I lost my boys just as suddenly as this," she said. "Billy and Tom went out together—they were killed at Saint-Éloi, but Frank came through it all to Vimy Ridge. Then the message came ... sudden too. One day I had him—then I lost him! Why shouldn't nice things come suddenly too—just like this!"

"You sure can have me—mother," the big fellow said.

The conductor was giving the last call. Then the boy took her in his arms and kissed her withered cheek, which took on a happy glow that made us all look the other way.

She and I stood together and watched the grinding wheels as they began to move. The spirit of youth, the indomitable, imperishable spirit of youth was in her eyes, and glowed in her withered face as she murmured happily,—

"I am one of the Next of Kin ... again, and my new boy is on that train."

We stood together until the train had gone from our sight.

"Let me see," I said, "how many chickens did you tell me that Biddy hen of yours had when the winter came?"

"Twenty-two," she laughed.

"Well," I said, "it's early yet."

"I just can't help it," she said seriously; "I have to be in it! After I got the word about my last boy, it seemed for a few days that I had come to the end of everything. I slept and slept and slept, just like you do when you've had company at your house,—the very nicest company, and they

79

go away!—and you're so lonely and idle, and tired, too, for you've been having such a good time you did not notice that you were getting near the edge. That's how I felt; but after a week I wanted to be working at something. I thought maybe the Lord had left my hands quite free so I could help some one else.... You have played croquet, haven't you? You know how the first person who gets out has the privilege of coming back a 'rover,' and giving a hand to any one. That's what I felt; I was a 'rover,' and you'd be surprised at all I have found to do. There are so many soldiers' wives with children who never get downtown to shop or see a play, without their children. I have lots to do in that line, and it keeps me from thinking.

"I want you to come with me now," she went on, "to see a woman who has something wrong with her that I can't find out. She has a sore thought. Her man has been missing since September, and is now officially reported killed. But there's something else bothering her."

"How do you know?" I asked.

She turned quickly toward me and said, "Have you any children?"

"Five," I said.

"Oh, well, then, you'll understand. Can't you tell by a child's cry whether it is hungry, or hurt, or just mad?"

"I can, I think," I said.

"Well, that's how I know. She's in deep grief over her husband, but there's more than that. Her eyes have a hurt look that I wish I could get out of them. You'll see it for yourself, and maybe we can get her to tell us. I just found her by accident last week—or at least, I found her; nothing happens by accident!"

We found her in a little faded green house, whose veranda was broken through in many places. Scared-looking, dark-eyed children darted shyly through the open door as we approached. In the darkened front room she received us, and, without any surprise, pleasure, or resentment in her voice, asked us to sit down. As our eyes became accustomed to the gloom, we wondered more and more why the sunshine was excluded, for there was no carpet to fade, nor any furniture which would have been injured. The most conspicuous object in the room was the framed family group taken just before "her man" went away. He was a handsome young fellow in his tidy uniform, and the woman beside him had such a merry face that I should never have known her for the sad and faded person who had met us at the door. In the picture she was smiling, happy, resolute; now her face was limp and frazzled, and had an indefinable challenge in it which baffled me. My old friend was right—there was a sore thought there!

The bright black eyes of the handsome soldier fascinated me; he was so much alive; so fearless; so confident, so brave,—so much needed by these little ones who clustered around his knee. Again, as I looked upon this picture, the horrors of war rolled over my helpless heart.

My old friend was trying hard to engage the woman in conversation, but her manner was abstracted and strange. I noticed her clothes were all black, even the flannel bandage around her throat—she was recovering from an attack of quinsy—was black too; and as if in answer to my thoughts, she said:—

"It was red—but I dyed it—I couldn't bear to have it red—it bothered me. That's why I keep the blinds down too—the sun hurts me—it has no right to shine—just the same as if nothing had happened." Her voice quivered with passion.

"Have you any neighbors, Mrs. C——?" I asked; for her manner made me uneasy—she had been too much alone.

"Neighbors!" she stormed,—"neighbors! I haven't any, and I do not want them: they would only lie about me—the way they lied about Fred!"

"Surely nobody ever lied about Fred," I said,—"this fine, brave fellow."

"He does look brave, doesn't he?" she cried. "You are a stranger, but you can see it, can't you? You wouldn't think he was a coward, would you?"

"I would stake everything on his bravery!" I said honestly, looking at the picture.

She came over and squeezed my hand.

"It was a wicked lie—all a lie!" she said bitterly.

"Tell us all about it," I said; "I am sure there has been a mistake."

She went quickly out of the room, and my old friend and I stared at each other without speaking. In a few minutes she came back with a "paper" in her hand, and, handing it to me, she said, "Read that and you'll see what they say!"

I read the announcement which stated that her husband had been missing since September 29, and was now believed to have been killed. "This is just what is sent to every one—" I began, but she interrupted me.

"Look here!" she cried, leaning over my shoulder and pointing to the two words "marginally noted"—"What does that mean?"

I read it over again:—

"We regret to inform you that the soldier marginally noted, who has been declared missing since September 29, is now believed to have been killed!"

81

"There!" she cried, "can't you see?" pointing again to the two words. "Don't you see what that means?—margin means the edge—and that means that Fred was noted for being always on the edge of the army, trying to escape, I suppose. But that's a lie, for Fred was not that kind, I tell you—he was no coward!"

I saw where the trouble lay, and tried to explain. She would not listen.

"Oh, but I looked in the dictionary and I know: 'margin' means 'the edge,' and they are trying to say that Fred was always edging off—you see—noted for being on the edge, that's what they say."

We reasoned, we argued, we explained, but the poor little lonely soul was obsessed with the idea that a deep insult had been put upon her man's memory.

Then my old friend had an idea. She opened her purse and brought out the notice which she had received of the death of her last boy.

We put the two notices side by side, and told her that these were printed by the thousands, and every one got the same. Just the name had to be filled in.

Then she saw it!

"Oh!" she cried, "I am so glad you showed me this, for I have been so bitter. I hated every one; it sounded so hard and cold and horrible—as if nobody cared. It was harder than losing Fred to have him so insulted. But now I see it all!"

"Isn't it too bad," said the old lady, as we walked home together, "that they do not have these things managed by women? Women would have sense enough to remember that these notices go to many classes of people—and would go a bit slow on the high-sounding phrases: they would say, 'The soldier whose name appears on the margin of this letter,' instead of 'The soldier who is marginally noted'; it might not be so concise, but it is a heap plainer. A few sentences of sympathy, too, and appreciation, written in by hand, would be a comfort. I tell you at a time like this we want something human, like the little girl who was put to bed in the dark and told that the angels would keep her company. She said she didn't want angels—she wanted something with a skin face!—So do we all! We are panicky and touchy, like a child that has been up too late the night before, and we have to be carefully handled. All the pores of our hearts are open and it is easy to get a chill!"

As we rode home in the car she told me about the letter which had come that day from her last boy:—

"It seemed queer to look at this letter and know that I would never get another one from the boys. Letters from the boys have been a big thing to me for many years. Billy and Tom were away from me for a long time

82

before the war, and they never failed to write. Frank was never away from me until he went over, and he was not much of a letter-writer,—just a few sentences! 'Hello, mother, how are you? I'm O.K. Hope you are the same. Sleeping well, and eating everything I can lay my hands on. The box came; it was sure a good one. Come again. So-long!' That was the style of Frank's letter. 'I don't want this poor censor to be boring his eyes out trying to find state secrets in my letters,' he said another time, apologizing for the shortness of it. 'There are lots of things that I would like to tell you, but I guess they will keep until I get home—I always could talk better than write.' ... But this letter is different. He seemed to know that he was going—west, as they say, and he wrote so seriously; all the boyishness had gone from him, and he seemed to be old, much older than I am. These boys of ours are all older than we are now,—they have seen so much of life's sadness—they have got above it; they see so many of their companions go over that they get a glimpse of the other shore. They are like very old people who cannot grieve the way younger people can at leaving this life."

Then I read the boy's letter.

"Dear Mother," it ran, "We are out resting now, but going in to-morrow to tackle the biggest thing that we have pulled off yet. You'll hear about it, I guess. Certainly you will if we are successful. I hope that this letter will go safely, for I want you to know just how I feel, and that everything is fine with me. I used to be scared stiff that I would be scared, but I haven't been—there seems to be something that stands by you and keeps your heart up, and with death all around you, you see it is not so terrible. I have seen so many of the boys pass out, and they don't mind it. They fight like wild-cats while they can, but when their turn comes they go easy. The awful roar of the guns does it. The silent tomb had a horrible sound to me when I was at home, but it sounds like a welcome now. Anyway, mother, whatever happens you must not worry. Everything is all right when you get right up to it—even death. I just wish I could see you, and make you understand how light-hearted I feel. I never felt better; my only trouble is that you will be worried about me, but just remember that everything is fine, and that I love you.

"Frank."

AT THE LAST!
O God, who hears the smallest cry That ever rose from human soul, Be near my mother when she reads My name upon the Honor Roll; And when she sees it written there, Dear Lord, stand to, behind her chair!

Or, if it be Thy sacred will That I may go and stroke her hand, Just let me say, "I'm living still! And in a brighter, better land." One word from me will cheer her so, O Lord, if you will let me go!

I know her eyes with tears will blind, I think I hear her choking cry, When in the list my name she'll find— Oh, let me—let me—let me try To somehow make her understand That it is not so hard to die!

She's thinking of the thirst and pain; She's thinking of the saddest things; She does not know an angel came And led me to the water-springs, She does not know the quiet peace That fell upon my heart like rain, When something sounded my release, And something eased the scorching pain. She does not know, I gladly went And am with Death, content, content.

I want to say I played the game— I played the game right to the end— I did not shrink at shot or flame, But when at last the good old friend, That some call Death, came beckoning me, I went with him, quite willingly! Just let me tell her—let her know— It really was not hard to go!

CHAPTER XIII
THE BELIEVING CHURCH

The gates of heaven are swinging open so often these days, as the brave ones pass in, that it would be a wonder if some gleams of celestial brightness did not come down to us.

We get it unexpectedly in the roar of the street; in the quiet of the midnight; in the sun-spattered aisles of the forest; in the faces of our friends; in the turbid stream of our poor burdened humanity. They shine out and are gone—these flashes of eternal truth. The two worlds cannot be far apart when the travel from one to the other is so heavy! No, I do not know what heaven is like, but it could not seem strange to me, for I know so many people now who are there! Sometimes I feel like the old lady who went back to Ontario to visit, and who said she felt more at home in the cemetery than anywhere else, for that is where most of her friends had gone!

These heavenly gleams have shown us new things in our civilization and in our social life, and most of all in our own hearts. Above all other lessons we have learned, or will learn, is the fallacy of hatred. Hatred weakens, destroys, disintegrates, scatters. The world's disease to-day is the withering, blighting, wasting malady of hatred, which has its roots in the narrow patriotism which teaches people to love their own country and despise all others. The superiority bug which enters the brain and teaches a nation that they are God's chosen people, and that all other nations must some day bow in obeisance to them, is the microbe which has poisoned the world. We must love our own country best, of course, just as we love our own children best; but it is a poor mother who does not desire the highest good for every other woman's child.

We are sick unto death of hatred, force, brutality; blood-letting will never bring about lasting results, for it automatically plants a crop of bitterness and a desire for revenge which start the trouble all over again. To kill a man does not prove that he was wrong, neither does it make converts of his friends. A returned man told me about hearing a lark sing one morning as the sun rose over the shell-scarred, desolated battlefield, with its smouldering piles of ruins which had once been human dwelling-places, and broken, splintered trees which the day before had been green and growing. Over this scene of horror, hatred, and death arose the lark into the morning air, and sang his glorious song. "And then," said the boy, as he steadied himself on his crutches, "he sang the very same song over again, just to show us that he could do it again and meant every word of it, and it gave me a queer feeling. It seemed to show me that the lark had the straight of it, and we were all wrong. But," he added, after a pause, "nobody knows how wrong it all is like the men who've been there!"

Of course we know that the world did not suddenly go wrong. Its thought must have been wrong all the time, and the war is simply the manifestation of it; one of them at least. But how did it happen? That is the question which weary hearts are asking all over the world. We all know what is wrong with Germany. That's easy. It is always easier to diagnose other people's cases than our own—and pleasanter. We know that the people of Germany have been led away by their teachers, philosophers, writers; they worship the god of force; they recognize no sin but weakness and inefficiency. They are good people, only for their own way of thinking; no doubt they say the same thing of us.

Wrong thinking has caused all our trouble, and the world cannot be saved by physical means, but only by the spiritual forces which change the mental attitude. When the sword shall be beaten into the ploughshare and the spear into the pruning-hook, that will be the outward sign of the change of thought from destructive, competitive methods to constructive and coöperative regeneration of the world! It is interesting to note that the sword and spear are not going to be thrown on the scrap-heap; they are to be transformed—made over. All energy is good; it is only its direction, which may become evil.

It is not to be wondered at that the world has run to blind hatred when we stop to realize that the Church has failed to teach the peaceable fruits of the spirit, and has preferred to fight human beings rather than prejudice, ignorance, and sin, and has too often gauged success by competition between its various branches, rather than by coöperation against the powers of evil.

At a recent convention of a certain religious body, one sister, who gave in her report as to how the Lord had dealt with the children of men in her part of the vineyard, deeply deplored the hardness of the sinners' hearts, their proneness to err, and the worldliness of even professing Christians, who seemed now to be wholly given over to the love of pleasure. She told also of the niggardly contributions; the small congregations. It was, indeed, a sad and discouraging tale that she unfolded. Only once did she show any enthusiasm, and that was in her closing words: "But I thank my Lord and Heavenly Master that the other church in our town ain't done no better!"

The Church is our oldest and best organization. It has enough energy, enough driving force, to better conditions for all if it could be properly applied; but being an exceedingly respectable institution it has been rather shy of changes, and so has found it hard to adapt itself to new conditions. It has clung to shadows after the substance has departed; and even holds to the old phraseology which belongs to a day long dead. Stately and beautiful and meaningful phrases they were, too, in their day, but now their fires are dead, their lights are out, their "punch" has departed. They are as pale and sickly as the red lanterns set to guard the spots of danger on the street at night and carelessly left burning all the next day.

Every decade sees the people's problems change, but the Church goes on with Balaam and Balak, with King Ahasuerus, and the two she-bears that came out of the woods. I shudder when I think of how much time has been spent in showing how Canaan was divided, and how little time is spent on showing how the Dominion of Canada should be divided; of how much time has been given to the man born blind, and how little to a

86

consideration of the causes and prevention of that blindness; of the time spent on our Lord's miraculous feeding of the five thousand, and how little time is spent on trying to find out his plans for feeding the hungry ones of to-day, who, we are bold to believe, are just as precious in his sight.

The human way is to shelve responsibility. The disciples came to Christ when the afternoon began to grow into evening, and said, "These people haven't anything to eat, send them away!" This is the human attitude toward responsibility; that is why many a beggar gets a quarter—and is told to "beat it"! In this manner are we able to side-step responsibility. To-day's problems are apt to lead to difficulties; it is safer to discuss problems of long ago than of the present; for the present ones concern real people, and they may not like it. Hush! Don't offend Deacon Bones; stick to Balaam—he's dead.

In some respects the Church resembles a coal furnace that has been burning quite a while without being cleaned out. There form in the bottom certain hard substances which give off neither light nor heat, nor allow a free current of air to pass through. These hard substances are called "clinkers." Once they were good pieces of burning coal, igniting the coal around them, but now their fire is dead, their heat is spent, and they must be removed for the good of the furnace. Something like this has happened in the Church. It has a heavy percentage of human "clinkers," sometimes in the front pews, sometimes in the pulpit. They were good people once, too, possessed of spiritual life and capable of inspiring those around them. But spiritual experiences cannot be warmed over—they must be new every day. That is what Saint Paul meant when he said that the outer man decays, but the inner man is renewed. An old experience in religion is of no more value than a last year's bird's nest! You cannot feed the hungry with last year's pot-pies!

This is the day of opportunity for the Church, for the people are asking to be led! It will have to realize that religion is a "here and now" experience, intended to help people with their human worries to-day, rather than an elaborate system of golden streets, big processions, walls of jasper, and endless years of listless loafing on the shores of the River of Life! The Church has directed too much energy to the business of showing people how to die and teaching them to save their souls, forgetting that one of these carefully saved souls is after all not worth much. Christ said, "He that saveth his life shall lose it!" and "He that loseth his life for my sake shall find it!" The soul can be saved only by self-forgetfulness. The monastery idea of retirement from the world in order that one may be sure of heaven is not a courageous way of meeting life's difficulties. But this plan of escape has been very popular even in

Protestant churches, as shown in our hymnology: "Why do we linger?" "We are but strangers here"; "Father, dear Father, take Thy children home"; "Earth is a wilderness, heaven is my home"; "I'm a pilgrim and a stranger"; "I am only waiting here to hear the summons, child, come home." These are some of the hymns with which we have beguiled our weary days of waiting; and yet, for all this boasted desire to be "up and away," the very people who sang these hymns have not the slightest desire to leave the "wilderness."

The Church must renounce the idea that, when a man goes forth to preach the Gospel, he has to consider himself a sort of glorified immigration agent, whose message is, "This way, ladies and gentlemen, to a better, brighter, happier world; earth is a poor place to stick around, heaven is your home." His mission is to teach his people to make of this world a better place—to live their lives here in such a way that other men and women will find life sweeter for their having lived. Incidentally we win heaven, but it must be a result, not an objective.

We know there is a future state, there is a land where the complications of this present world will be squared away. Some call it a Day of Judgment; I like best to think of it as a day of explanations. I want to hear God's side. Also I know we shall not have to lie weary centuries waiting for it. When the black curtain of death falls on life's troubled scenes, there will appear on it these words in letters of gold, "End of Part I. Part II will follow immediately."

I know that I shall have a sweet and beautiful temper in heaven, where there will be nothing to try it, no worries, misunderstandings, elections, long and tedious telephone conversations; people who insist on selling me a dustless mop when I am hot on the trail of an idea. There will be none of that, so that it will not be difficult to keep sweet and serene. I would not thank any one to hand me a sword and shield when the battle is over; I want it now while the battle rages; I claim my full equipment now, not on merit, but on need.

Everything in life encourages me to believe that God has provided a full equipment for us here in life if we will only take it. He would not store up every good thing for the future and let us go short here.

In a prosperous district in Ontario there stands a beautiful brick house, where a large family of children lived long ago. The parents worked early and late, grubbing and saving and putting money in the bank. Sometimes the children resented the hard life which they led, and wished for picnics, holidays, new clothes, ice-cream, and the other fascinating things of childhood. Some of the more ambitious ones even craved a higher education, but they were always met by the same answer when the request involved the expenditure of money. The answer was: "It will all be yours some day. Now, don't worry; just let us work together and save all we can; it's all for you children and it will all be yours some day. You can do what you like with it when we are dead and gone!" I suppose the children in their heart of hearts said, "Lord haste the day!"

The parents passed on in the fullness of time. Some of the children went before them. Those who were left fell heir to the big house and the beautiful grounds, but they were mature men and women then, and they had lost the art of enjoyment. The habit of saving and grubbing was upon them, and their aspirations for better things had long ago died out. Everything had been saved for the future, and now, when it came, they found out that it was all too late. The time for learning and enjoyment had gone by. A few dollars spent on them when they were young would have done so much.

If that is a poor policy for earthly parents to follow, I believe it is not a good line for a Heavenly Parent to take.

We need an equipment for this present life which will hold us steady even when everything around us is disturbed; that will make us desire the good of every one, even those who are intent upon doing us evil; that will transform the humblest and most disagreeable task into one of real pleasure; that will enable us to see that we have set too high a value on the safety of life and property and too trifling an estimate on spiritual things; that will give us a proper estimate of our own importance in the general scheme of things, so that we will not think we are a worm in the dust, nor yet mistake ourselves for the President of the Company!

The work of the Church is to teach these ethical values to the people. It must begin by teaching us to have more faith in each other, and more coördination. We cannot live a day without each other, and every day we become more interdependent. Times have changed since the cave-dwelling days when every man was his own butcher, baker, judge, jury, and executioner; when no man attempted more than he could do alone, and therefore regarded every other man as his natural enemy and rival, the killing of whom was good business. Coöperation began when men found that two men could hunt better than one, and so one drove the bear out of the cave and the other one killed him as he went past the gap, and then divided him, fifty-fifty. That was the beginning of coöperation, which is built on faith. Strange, isn't it, that at this time, when we need each other so badly, we are not kinder to each other? Our national existence depends upon all of us—we have pooled our interests, everything we have is in danger, everything we have must be mobilized for its defense.

89

Danger such as we are facing should drive the petty little meannesses out of us, one would think, and call out all the latent heroism of our people. People talk about this being the Church's day of opportunity. So it is, for the war is teaching us ethical values, which has always been a difficult matter. We like things that we can see, lay out, and count! But the war has changed our appraisement of things, both of men and of nations. A country may be rich in armies, ships, guns, and wealth, and yet poor, naked, and dishonored in the eyes of the world; a country may be broken, desolate, shell-riven, and yet have a name that is honorable in all the earth. So with individuals. We have set too high a value on property and wealth, too low an estimate on service.

Our ideas of labor have been wrong. Labor to us has meant something disagreeable, which, if we endure patiently for a season, we may then be able to "chuck." Its highest reward is to be able to quit it—to go on the retired list.

"Mary married well," declared a proud mother, "and now she does not lift a hand to anything."

Poor Mary! What a slow time she must have!

The war is changing this; people are suddenly stripped of their possessions, whether they be railroad stock, houses, or lands, or, like that of a poor fellow recently tried for vagrancy here, whose assets were found to be a third interest in a bear. It does not matter—the wealthy slacker is no more admired than the poor one. Money has lost its purchasing quality when it comes to immunity from responsibility.

The coördination of our people has begun, the forces of unity are working; but they are still hindered by the petty little jealousies and disputes of small people who do not yet understand the seriousness of the occasion. So long as church bodies spend time fighting about methods of baptism, and call conventions to pass resolutions against church union, which would unquestionably add to the effectiveness of the Church and enable it to make greater headway against the powers of evil; so long as the channels through which God's love should flow to the people are so choked with denominational prejudice, it is not much wonder that many people are experiencing a long, dry spell, bitterly complaining that the fountain has gone dry. Love, such as Christ demonstrated, is the only hope of this sin-mad world. When the Church shows forth that love and leads the people to see that the reservoirs of love in the mountains of God are full to overflowing, and every man can pipe the supply into his own heart and live victoriously, abundantly, gloriously, as God intended us all to live, then it will come about that the sword will be beaten into the

The Next of Kin: Those who Wait and Wonder

ploughshare and the spear into the pruning-hook, and the Lord will truly hear our prayer and heal our land.

CHAPTER XIV
THE LAST RESERVES

To-day I read in one of our newspapers an account of a religious convention which is going on in our city. It said that one of the lady delegates asked if, in view of the great scarcity of men to take the various fields, and the increased number of vacancies, the theological course in their colleges would be opened to women? And the report said, "A ripple of amusement swept over the convention."

I know that ripple. I know it well! The Church has always been amused when the advancement of women has been mentioned right out boldly like that. There are two things which have never failed to bring a laugh— a great, round, bold oath on the stage, and any mention of woman suffrage in the pulpit. They have been sure laugh-producers. When we pray for the elevation of the stage in this respect, we should not forget the Church!

I have been trying to analyze that ripple of amusement. Here is the situation: The men have gone out to fight. The college halls are empty of boys, except very young ones. One of the speakers at the same session said, "We do not expect to get in boys of more than eighteen years of age." Churches are closed for lack of preachers. What is to be done about it? No longer can Brother M. be sent to England to bring over pink-cheeked boys to fill the ranks of Canada's preachers. The pink-cheeked ones are also "over there." There is no one to call upon but women. So why was the suggestion of the lady delegate received with amusement? Why was it not acted upon? For although there were many kind and flattering things said about women, their great services to Church and State, yet the theological course was not opened.

The Church has been strangely blind in its attitude toward women, and with many women it will be long remembered with a feeling of bitterness that the Church has been so slow to move.

The Government of the Western Provinces of Canada gave full equality to women before that right was given by the Church. The Church has not given it yet. The Church has not meant to be either unjust or unkind, and the indifference and apathy of its own women members have given the unthinking a reason for their attitude. Why should the vote be forced on women? they have asked. It is quite true that the women of the Church have not said much, for the reason that many of the brightest women, on account of the Church's narrowness, have withdrawn and gone elsewhere, where more liberty could be found. This is unfortunate, and I think a mistake on the part of the women. Better to have stayed and fought it out than to go out slamming the door.

Many sermons have I listened to in the last quarter of a century of fairly regular church attendance; once I heard an Englishman preaching bitterly of the Suffragettes' militant methods, and he said they should all "be condemned to motherhood to tame their wild spirits." And I surely had the desire to slam the door that morning, for I thought I never heard a more terrible insult to all womankind than to speak of motherhood as a punishment. But I stayed through the service; I stayed after the service! I interviewed the preacher. So did many other women! He had a chastened spirit when we were through with him.

I have listened to many sermons that I did not like, but I possessed my soul in patience. I knew my turn would come—it is a long lane that has no tomato-cans! My turn did come—I was invited to address the conference of the Church, and there with all the chief offenders lined up in black-coated, white-collared rows, I said all that was in my heart, and they were honestly surprised. One good old brother, who I do not think had listened to a word that I said, arose at the back of the church and said: "I have listened to all that this lady has had to say, but I am not convinced. I have it on good authority that in Colorado, where women vote, a woman once stuffed a ballot-box. How can the lady explain that?" I said I could explain it, though, indeed, I could not see that it needed any explanation. No one could expect women to live all their lives with men without picking up some of their little ways! That seemed to hold the brother for a season!

The Church's stiff attitude toward women has been a hard thing to explain to the "world." Many a time I have been afraid that it would be advanced as a reason for not considering woman suffrage in the State. "If the Church," politicians might well have said, "with its spiritual understanding of right and justice, cannot see its way clear to give the vote to women, why should the State incur the risk?" Whenever I have invited questions, at the close of an address, I have feared that one. That cheerful air of confidence with which I urged people to speak right up and ask any question they wished always covered a trembling and fearful heart. You have heard of people whistling as they passed a graveyard, and perhaps you thought that they were frivolously light-hearted? Oh, no! That is not why they whistled!

When the vote was given to the women in our province and all the other Western provinces, I confess that I thought our worst troubles were over. I see now that they were really beginning. A second Hindenburg line has been set up, and seems harder to pierce than the first. It is the line of bitter prejudice! Some of those who, at the time the vote was given, made eloquent speeches of welcome, declaring their long devotion to the cause of women, are now busily engaged in trying to make it uncomfortably hot for the women who dare to enter the political field. They are like the employers who furnish seats for their clerks in the stores, yet make it clear that to use them may cost their jobs.

The granting of the franchise to women in western Canada, was brought about easily. It won, not by political pressure, but on its merits. There is something about a new country which beats out prejudice, and the pioneer age is not so far removed as to have passed out of memory. The real men of the West remember gratefully how the women stood by them in the old hard days, taking their full share of the hardships and the sacrifice uncomplainingly. It was largely this spirit which prompted the action of the legislators of the West. As Kipling says:—

Now and not hereafter, while the breath is in our nostrils, Now and not hereafter, ere the meaner years go by, Let us now remember many honorable women— They who stretched their hands to us, when we were like to die!

There was not any great opposition here in western Canada. One member did say that, if women ever entered Parliament, he would immediately resign; but the women were not disturbed. They said that it was just another proof of the purifying effect that the entrance of women into politics would have! Sitting in Parliament does not seem like such a hard job to those of us who have sat in the Ladies' Gallery and looked over; there is such unanimity among members of Parliament, such remarkable and unquestioning faith in the soundness of their party's opinion. In one of the Parliaments of the West there sat for twelve years an honored member who never once broke the silence of the back benches except to say, "Aye," when he was told to say, "Aye." But on toward the end of the thirteenth year he gave unmistakable signs of life.

A window had been left open behind him, and when the draft blew over him—he sneezed! Shortly after, he got up and shut the window!

Looking down upon such tranquil scenes as these there are women who have said in their boastful way that they believe they could do just as well—with a little practice!

Women who sit in Parliament will do so by sheer merit, for there is still enough prejudice to keep them out if any reason for so doing can be found. Their greatest contribution, in Parliament and out of it, will be independence of thought.

Women have not the strong party affiliations which men have. They have no political past, no political promises to keep, no political sins to expiate. They start fair and with a clean sheet. Those who make the mistake of falling into old party lines, and of accepting ready-made opinions and prejudices, will make no difference in the political life of the country except to enlarge the voters' list and increase the expenses of elections.

Just now partyism is falling into disfavor, for there are too many serious questions to be fought out. There are still a few people who would rather lose the war than have their party defeated, but not many. "When the Empire is in danger is no time to think of men," appeals to the average thinking man and woman. The independent man who carefully thinks out issues for himself, and who is not led away by election cries, is the factor who has held things steady in the past. Now it seems that this independent body will be increased by the new voters, and if so, they will hold in their hands the balance of power in any province, and really become a terror to evil-doers as well as a praise to those who do well!

Old things are passing away, and those who have eyes to see it know that all things are becoming new. The political ideals of the far-off, easy days of peace will not do for these new and searching times. Political ideals have been different from any other. Men who would not rob a bank or sandbag a traveler, and who are quite punctilious about paying their butcher and their baker, have been known to rob the country quite freely and even hilariously, doctoring an expense sheet, overcharging for any service rendered. "Good old country," they have seemed to say, "if I do not rob you, some one else will!"

This easy conscience regarding the treasury of the country is early shown in the attitude toward road-work, those few days' labor which the municipality requires men to do as part payment of their taxes. Who has not noticed the languorous ease of the lotus-eating road-workers as they sit on their plough-handles and watch the slow afternoon roll by?

Politics too long has been a mystical word which has brought visions of a dark but fascinating realm of romantic intrigue, sharp deals, good-natured tricks, and lucky strikes. The greatest asset a politician can have is the ability to "put it over" and "get something for us." The attitude of the average voter has been that of expectancy. If he renders a public service, he expects to be remunerated. His relation to his country has not been, "What can I do?" but, "What can I get?" His hand has been outstretched palm upward! Citizenship to us has not meant much; it has come too easy, like money to the rich man's son! All things have been ours by inheritance—free speech, freedom of religion, responsible government. Somebody fought for these things, but it was a long time ago, and only in a vague way are we grateful! These things become valuable only when threatened.

There hangs on the wall, in one of the missions in the city of Winnipeg, a picture of a street in one of the Polish villages. In it the people are huddled together, cowering with fear. The priest, holding aloft the sacred crucifix, stands in front of them, while down the street come the galloping Cossacks with rifles and bayonets. Polish men and women have cried bitter tears before that picture. They knew what happened. They knew that the sacred sign of the crucifix did not stay the fury of the Cossacks! These are the people, these Polish people, who have been seen to kiss the soil of Canada in an ecstasy of gladness when they set foot upon it, for it is to them the land of liberty. Liberty of speech and of action, safety of life and of property mean something to them; but we have always enjoyed these things, and esteem them lightly.

The first blow between the eyes that our complacency received was Belgium!—that heroic little country to whose people citizenship was so much dearer than life or riches, or even the safety of their loved ones, that they flung all these things away, in a frenzy of devotion, for the honor of their country and her good name among nations. This has disturbed us: we cannot forget Belgium. It has upset our comfortable Canadian conscience, for it has given us a glimpse of the upper country, and life can never be the same again. It is not all of life to live—that is, grow rich and quit work.

The heroism of the trenches is coming back to us. It is filtering through. It is the need for heroism which is bringing it out. We are playing a losing game, even though we are winning. There is only one thing more disastrous than a victory, and that is a defeat. I do not need to enumerate what we are losing—we know. What can we do to make good the loss? Some of our people have always done all they could: they have always stood in the front trench and "carried on"; others have been in the "stand-to" trench, and have done well, too, in time of stress. Many have not yet signed on, but they will: they are not cowards, they are only indifferent. This has been true of the protected woman in the home, who has not considered herself a citizen.

We have come to the place now when our full force must be called out. The women are our last reserves. If they cannot heal the world, we are lost, for they are the last we have—we cannot call the angels down. The trumpets are calling now in every street of every town, in every country lane, even in the trackless fastnesses of the North Country. The call is for citizens,—woman citizens,—who, with deft and skillful fingers, will lovingly, patiently undertake the task of piecing together the torn mantle of civilization; who will make it so strong, so beautiful, so glorified, that never again can it be torn or soiled or stained with human blood. The trumpets are calling for healers and binders who will not be appalled at the task of nursing back to health a wounded world, shot to pieces by injustice, greed, cruelty, and wrong thinking.

The sign of the Red Cross is a fitting emblem for the Order, worn not only on the sleeve, but in the heart; red to remind its wearer that God made all people of one blood, and is the Father of all; and the Cross which speaks of the One whose mission on earth was to save; who came not to be ministered unto, but to minister. Every one who signs on does so for "duration," and must consider herself under orders until the coming in of that glad day

"When men shall brothers be And form one family The wide world o'er!"

CHAPTER XV
LIFE'S TRAGEDY

It often happens that people die At the hand of that they loved the best; One who loves horses all his days By a horse's hoof is laid to rest!

The swimmer who loves on the waves to lie Is caught in the swell of a passing boat, And the thing he loves breaks over his head And chokes the breath from his gasping throat.

And the Christ who loved all men so well That he came to earth their friend to be, By one was denied, by one betrayed, By others nailed to the cursèd tree!

And more and more I seem to see That Love is the world's great Tragedy!

Love is a terrible thing—quite different from amiability, which is sometimes confused with it. Amiability will never cause people to do hard things, but love will tear the heart to pieces!

It was because the people of Belgium loved their country that they chose to suffer all things rather than have her good name tarnished among the nations of the earth. It has been for love, love of fair play, love of British traditions, that Canada has sent nearly four hundred thousand men across the sea to fight against the powers of darkness. Canada has nothing to gain in this struggle, in a material way, as a nation, and even less has there been any chance of gain to the individual who answered the call. There are many things that may happen to the soldier after he has put on the uniform, but sudden riches is not among them.

Some of the men, whose love of country made them give up all and follow the gleam, have come back to us now, and on pleasant afternoons may be seen sitting on the balconies of the Convalescent Homes or perhaps being wheeled in chairs by their more fortunate companions. Their neighbors, who had an amiable feeling for the country instead of love, and who therefore stayed at home, are very sorry for these broken men, and sometimes, when the day is fine, they take the "returned men" out in their big cars for a ride!

There are spiritual and moral dead-beats in every community who get through life easily by following a "safety-first" plan in everything, who keep close to the line of "low visibility," which means, "Keep your head down or you may get hit"; who allow others to do the fighting and bear all the criticism, and then are not even gracious enough to acknowledge the unearned benefits. The most popular man in every community is the one who has never taken a stand on any moral question; who has never loved anything well enough to fight for it; who is broad-minded and tolerant—because he does not care.... Amiability fattens, but love kills!

Amiable patriots at the present time talk quite cheerfully of the conscription of life, but say little of the conscription of wealth, declaring quite truthfully that wealth will never win the war! Neither will men! It will take both, and all we have, too, I am afraid. Surely if the government feels that it can ask one man for his life, it need not be so diffident about

97

asking another man for his wealth. The conscription of wealth might well begin with placing all articles of food and clothing on the free list and levying a direct tax on all land values. Then, if all profits from war-supplies were turned over to the government, there would be money enough to pay a fair allowance to our soldiers and their dependents. It does not seem fair that the soldier should bear all the sacrifices of hardship and danger, and then have the additional one of poverty for his family and the prospect of it for himself, when he comes back unfit for his former occupation. Hardship and danger for the soldier are inevitable, but poverty is not. The honest conscription of wealth would make it possible for all who serve the Empire to have an assurance of a decent living as long as they live.

If equal pay were given to every man, whether he is a private or a major, equal pensions to every soldier's widow, and if all political preference were eliminated, as it would have to be under this system; when all service is put on the same basis and one man's life counts as much as another's, there would be no need of compulsion to fill the ranks of the Canadian army. We know that there never can be equality of service—the soldier will always bear the heavy burden, and no money can ever pay him for what he does; but we must not take refuge behind that statement to let him bear the burdens which belong to the people who stay at home.

Heroism is contagious. It becomes easier when every one is practicing it. What we need now, more than anything, are big, strong, heroic leaders, men of moral passion, who will show us the hard path of sacrifice, not asking us to do what they are not willing to do themselves; not pointing the way, but traveling in it; men of heroic mould who will say, "If my right eye offend me, I will pluck it out"; men who are willing to go down to political death if the country can be saved by that sacrifice. We need men at home who are as brave as the boys in the trenches, who risk their lives every day in a dozen different ways, without a trace of self-applause, who have laid all their equipment on the altar of sacrifice; who "carry on" when all seems hopeless; who stand up to death unflinchingly, and at the last, ask only, that their faces may be turned to the West!—to Canada!

We have always had plenty of amiability, but in this terrible time it will not do. Our country is calling for love.

CHAPTER XVI
WAITING!

Sing a song of the Next of Kin, A weary, wishful, waiting rhyme, That has no tune and has no time, But just a way of wearing in!

Sing a song of those who weep While slow the weary night hours go; Wondering if God willed it so, That human life should be so cheap!

Sing a song of those who wait, Wondering what the post will bring; Saddened when he slights the gate, Trembling at his ring,—

The day the British mail comes in Is a day of thrills for the Next of Kin.

When the Alpine climbers make a dangerous ascent, they fasten a rope from one to the other; so that if one slips, the others will be able to hold him until he finds his feet again; and thus many a catastrophe is averted! We have a ring like that here—we whose boys are gone. Somebody is almost sure to get a letter when the British mail comes in; and even a letter from another boy read over the 'phone is cheering, especially if he mentions your boy—or even if he doesn't; for we tell each other that the writer of the letter would surely know "if anything had happened."

Even "Posty" does his best to cheer us when the letters are far apart, and when the British mail has brought us nothing tells us it was a very small, and, he is sure, divided mail, and the other part of it will be along to-morrow. He also tells us the U-boats are probably accounting for the scarcity of French mail, anyway, and we must not be worried. He is a good fellow, this "Posty"!

We hold tight to every thread of comfort—we have to. That's why we wear bright-colored clothes: there is a buoyancy, an assurance about them, that we sorely need! We try to economize on our emotions, too, never shedding a useless or idle tear! In the days of peace we could afford to go to see "East Lynne," "Madame X," or "Romeo and Juliet," and cry our eyes red over their sorrows. Now we must go easy on all that! Some of us are running on the emergency tank now, and there is still a long way to go!

There are some things we try not to think about, especially at night. There is no use—we have thought it all over and over again; and now our

99

brains act like machines which have been used for sewing something too heavy for them, and which don't "feed" just right, and skip stitches. So we try to do the things that we think ought to be done, and take all the enjoyment we can from the day's work.

We have learned to divide our time into day-lengths, following the plan of the water-tight compartments in ships, which are so arranged that, if a leak occurs in one of these, the damaged one may be closed up, and no harm is done to the ship. So it is in life. We can live so completely one day at a time that no mournful yesterday can throw its dull shadow on the sunshine of to-day; neither can any frowning to-morrow reach back and with a black hand slap its smiling face. To-day is a sacred thing if we know how to live it.

I am writing this on the fourth day of August, which is a day when memory grows bitter and reflective if we are not careful. The August sunshine lies rich and yellow on the fields, and almost perceptibly the pale green of the wheat is absorbing the golden hue of the air. The painted cup has faded from rosy pink to a dull, ashy color, and the few wild roses which are still to be seen in the shaded places have paled to a pastel shade. The purple and yellow of goldenrod, wild sage, gallardia, and coxcomb are to be seen everywhere—the strong, bold colors of the harvest.

Everything spoke of peace to-day as we drove through the country. The air had the indescribably sweet smell of ripening grain, clover-blooms, and new hay; for the high stands of wild hay around the ponds and lakes are all being cut this year, and even the timothy along the roads, and there was a mellow undertone of mowing machines everywhere, like the distant hum of a city. Fat cattle stood knee-deep in a stream as we passed, and others lay contentedly on the clover-covered banks. One restless spirit, with a poke on her neck, sniffed at us as we went by, and tossed her head in grim defiance of public opinion and man-made laws. She had been given a bad name—and was going to live up to it!

Going over a hill, we came upon a woman driving a mower. It was the first reminder of the war. She was a fine-looking woman, with a tanned face, brown, but handsome, and she swung her team around the edge of the meadow with a grace and skill that called forth our admiration.

I went over and spoke to her, for I recognized her as a woman whom I had met at the Farm-Woman's Convention last winter. After we had exchanged greetings, and she had made her kind inquiry, "What news do you get from the Front?" and had heard that my news had been good—she said abruptly:—

"Did you know I've lost my husband?"

I expressed my sorrow.

"Yes," she said, "it was a smashing blow—never believed Alex could be killed: he was so big, and strong, and could do anything.... Ever since I can remember, I thought Alex was the most wonderful of all people on earth ... and at first ... when the news came, it seemed I could not go on living ... but I am all right now, and have thought things out.... This isn't the only plane of existence ... there are others; this is merely one phase of life.... I am taking a longer view of things now.... You see that schoolhouse over there,"—she pointed with her whip to a green-and-white school farther down the road,—"Alex and I went to school there.... We began the same day and left the same day. His family and mine settled in this neighborhood twenty years ago—we are all Kincardine people—Bruce, you know. Our road to school lay together on the last mile ... and we had a way of telling whether the other one had passed. We had a red willow stick which we drove into the ground. Then, when I came along in the morning and found it standing, I knew I was there first. I pulled it out and laid it down, so when Alex came he knew I had passed, and hurried along after me. When he came first and found it standing, he always waited for me, if he could, for he would rather be late than go without me. When I got the message I could not think of anything but the loneliness of the world, for a few days; but after a while I realized what it meant ... Alex had passed ... the willow was down ... but he'll wait for me some place ... nothing is surer than that! I am not lonely now.... Alex and I are closer together than plenty of people who are living side by side. Distance is a matter of spirit ... like everything else that counts.

"I am getting on well. The children are at school now, both of them,—they sit in the same seats we sat in,—the crops are in good shape—did you ever see a finer stand of wild hay? I can manage the farm, with one extra hired man in harvest-time. Alex went out on the crest of the wave—he had just been recommended for promotion—the children will always have a proud memory.

"This is a great country, isn't it? Where can you find such abundance, and such a climate, with its sunshine and its cool nights, and such a chance to make good?... I suppose freedom has to be paid for. We thought the people long ago had paid for it, but another installment of the debt fell due. Freedom is like a farm—it has to be kept up. It is worth something to have a chance to work and bring up my children—in peace—so I am living on from day to day ... not grieving ... not moping ... not thinking too much,—it hurts to think too hard,—just living."

Then we shook hands, and I told her that she had found something far greater than happiness, for she had achieved power!

There is a fine rainbow in the sky this evening, so bright and strong that it shows again in a reflected bow on the clouds behind it. A rainbow is a heartsome thing, for it reminds us of a promise made long ago, and faithfully kept.

There is shadow and shine, sorrow and joy, all the way along. This is inevitable, and so we must take them as they come, and rejoice over every sunny hour of every day, or, if the day is all dark, we must go hopefully forward through the gloom.

To-day has been fine. There was one spattering shower, which pebbled the dusty roads, and a few crashes of rolling thunder. But the western sky is red now, giving promise of a good day to-morrow.

A PRAYER FOR THE NEXT OF KIN

O Thou, who once Thine own Son gave To save the world from sin, Draw near in pity now we crave To all the Next of Kin. To Thee we make our humble prayer To save us from despair!

Send sleep to all the hearts that wake; Send tears into the eyes that burn; Steady the trembling hands that shake; Comfort all hearts that mourn. But most of all, dear Lord, we pray For strength to see us through this day.

As in the wilderness of old, When Thou Thy children safely led, They gathered, as we have been told, One day's supply of heavenly bread, And if they gathered more than that, At evening it was stale and flat,—

So, Lord, may this our faith increase— To leave, untouched, to-morrow's load, To take of grace a one-day lease Upon life's winding road. Though round the bend we may not see, Still let us travel hopefully!

Or, if our faith is still so small— Our hearts so void of heavenly grace, That we may still affrighted be In passing some dark place— Then in Thy mercy let us run Blindfolded in the race.

THE END

Made in the USA
Monee, IL
08 July 2021